Praise for **Between Wounded and Well**

Vincent J. Felitti, MD, Co-investigator of The Adverse Childhood Experience (ACE) Study, CA "It is my honor to recommend *Between Wounded and Well: Lessons in Healing* to all who seek a deeper understanding of trauma, recovery, and the extraordinary resilience of the human spirit. It will inspire those still navigating their own journeys from wounded to well."

Mimi Secor, DNP, Nurse Practitioner, Author, Coach, Recipient of 2025 Sharp Cutting- Edge Award, AANP, MA "*Between Wounded and Well: Lessons in Healing* by Dr. Debra Palmer is a profoundly personal and universally relevant story about resilience. It is a testament to the power of storytelling, perseverance, faith and hope. Her story is sure to teach, empower and inspire the reader. I highly recommend it."

Rosemary Goodyear, Ed.D., Nurse Practitioner, Consultant in International Nursing Program and Policy Development, CA "*Between Wounded and Well* is an outstanding contribution to assist individuals when encountering social, physical and psychological challenges, providing a foundation for the healing process."

Casey Gwinn, JD, President of Alliance for HOPE International, "Debra Palmer writes with authenticity and transparency about a journey most survivors are never willing so share. Many others who have survived abuse or are caring for those who have survived can benefit from her lessons learned. Hope can heal trauma and pain can become power; Debra is a living, breathing testimony to both."

Rev. Rebekah Simon-Peter, Author and Developer of Creating a Culture of Renewal, WY "Debra Palmer writes in vivid detail about her experiences and shares powerful insights about moving from wounded to well, emotionally, physically, relationally, and spiritually. An inspiring read."

Eileen K. Fry-Bowers, PhD, JD , Dean and Professor, University of San Francisco, School of Nursing and Health Professions "In *Between Wounded and Well: Lessons in Healing,* Dr. Deb Palmer shares her story in an authentic and poignant manner, recounting in vivid detail, how her life was shaped by adverse childhood experiences and generational trauma. I am certain that her story will be a light for others. Remarkably, her story is one of growth, acceptance and hope, told in a way that only a nurse can tell."

Erin Shree Vaghn, LCSW, FLA "Debra's book offers a unique and informative voice, grounded in deep medical expertise conveyed with clarity and compassion any reader could understand and relate to. Debra skillfully weaves faith into the discussion of healing, offering a holistic and empathetic perspective. It's both accessible and profoundly insightful."

Valerie Costa, Author, Editor and Coach, VA "In *Between Wounded and Well* I loved how raw and real Debra was in telling her story. I laughed and cried a few times, and she gave me food-for-thought about my own difficult relationships."

Susan Instone, DNS, Pediatric Nurse practitioner, CA "Dr. Palmer weaves a heart wrenching story about trauma, loss, and perseverance to become a gifted nurse practitioner and mentor for the next generation. Her journey is inspiring!"

Anne Walsh, Adult Nurse Practitioner, Wound care Specialist and founder of Wound Care Pro APP, NY "I loved the relationship to the wound healing stages. It was very inspiring and will be great for others to read, be inspired and empowered! Amazing accomplishments through tough situations. I thought it was well written and a wonderful tribute to your family. Congratulations!!!!"

BETWEEN WOUNDED

WOUNDED

and **WELL**

BETWEEN
WOUNDED
and WELL

a Nurse Practitioner Memoir

DEBRA PALMER, PhD

Published by Palmer Aces 4 Wellness
WWW.DebraPalmer.com
Windsor, California

ISBN (paperback): 979-8-9985577-0-5
ISBN (ebook): 979-8-9985577-1-2

Book design and production by www.AuthorSuccess.com

Printed in the United States of America

Disclaimer
The events in this memoir are accurate to the best of the author's memory. Events, locations, and conversations have been recreated from memory. To protect the privacy and identity of certain parties, the names of individuals, employers, and locations have been changed. The author in no way represents any company, corporation, or brand mentioned herein. The views expressed in this memoir are solely those of the author, as a storyteller for inspiration purposes only. Nothing in the book should be taken as medical advice. Consult qualified healthcare professionals regarding medical or psychological concerns or treatment decisions.

Dedication

This book is dedicated to the Divine Creator, my life partner, and all the past and present nurses in my life.

CONTENTS

FOREWORD

BY VINCENT J. FELITTI, MD

Co-Principal Investigator,

The Adverse Childhood Experience (ACE) Study

Over the past several decades, the growing field of trauma research has revealed an undeniable truth: What happens to us in childhood can echo across a lifetime, shaping our physical health, our emotional well-being and our behaviors in ways that are both profound and for many, unrecognized. While data from the adverse childhood experience (ACE) study helped illuminate the public health implications of this reality, the personal stories behind the data are what truly bring science to life.

Doctor Debra Palmer's *Between Wounded and Well: Lessons in Healing* is one such story, told with clarity, humility, and remarkable insight. In this personal and professionally grounded memoir, Doctor Palmer shares her journey from childhood marked by adversity to a life of service, purpose, and healing as a nurse practitioner and educator. Her story is not just one of survival, but of transformation.

What distinguishes this book is its unique structure: Doctor Palmer organizes her narrative around the four physiological stages of wound healing, mirroring the emotional and spiritual phases of her own recovery. This framework offers readers a multidimensional understanding of healing that respects the mind, and body. It is an especially powerful model for health care professionals, educators, and trauma survivors alike.

In my work, I have often seen how people with unresolved childhood trauma struggle silently, unaware of how their early experiences are influencing their behaviors and long-term health. Doctor Palmer's honest reflections provide both context and hope. She does not shy away from pain, nor does she dwell in it. Instead, she offers the reader a road map grounded in faith, informed by science, and animated with hard-won wisdom.

Her voice is especially needed at a time when our systems of care are being called to become more trauma informed, more compassionate, and more inclusive of the whole person. Through her story, Doctor Palmer affirms that healing is possible clinically, and at the deepest human level, once a person acknowledges and understands their own development and experiences.

It is my honor to recommend *Between Wounded and Well: Lessons in Healing* to all who seek a deeper understanding of trauma, recovery, and the extraordinary resilience of the human spirit. It will inspire those still navigating their own journeys from wounded to well.

Vincent J. Felitti, MD
Clinical Professor of Medicine, University of California
Founder, Department of Preventive Medicine, Kaiser Permanente, San Diego, CA
Co-Principal Investigator, Adverse Childhood Experience (Ace) Study

INTRODUCTION

Duluth, Minnesota

In the summer of 1976, I was nineteen, divorced with a four-year-old son, and working night shifts as a licensed practical nurse. While standing in line waiting to cash a check at Shopper City, my thoughts were interrupted by a tap on my shoulder. I abruptly swiveled to see who was behind me and immediately recognized Steve, a guy I had a crush on in sixth-grade Sunday School.

"Wow, I haven't seen you since . . ."

"Last summer at the hospital," he interrupted, flashing his charismatic smile.

"Yeah, in the cafeteria, my last week of nurses' training. What are you doing here? I thought you moved to Indiana to go to college."

"I'm working as a security guard for the summer. I saw you walking into the store from up there with binoculars," he said, pointing to the balcony, "So I followed you. I knew I'd eventually run into you since you live nearby."

I nodded and started to say something when he interrupted me. "Oh, you're engaged?" he asked, surprised, as he glanced at my left hand.

In that instant, the noise of the overhead paging system, crying babies, and chatter faded as thoughts and emotions competed for the attention of my subconscious mind. In less time than the blink of an eye, I had an epiphany. Being engaged to Will, an unemployed pothead, was a mistake. Initially, I was attracted to his caring nature, and as a single parent, I wanted to help him with his daughter while he looked for a job. Six months later, I felt more invested in his job search than he did, and that wasn't my responsibility. Yet, I took on the challenge as though it were. Steve's appearance triggered the realization that I wanted someone more relatable, with a work ethic and similar values.

In an instant, I reached with my right hand to remove the engagement ring from my left ring finger and slipped the ring into the right front pocket of my favorite hip-hugger jeans and swung my long, bleached-blond hair over my right shoulder, locked eyes with Steve, and replied, "Not anymore."

The gift of Steve's presence that fateful day was a reminder of what I wanted in a partner, and my fiancé was not that person. What remarkable timing, like the day at church when Steve said, "You should really break up with that guy, he's too old for you."

That guy became the father of my son when I was fourteen. Back then, I brushed Steve's concerns away, but now the problems that popped into my head as I stood in front of him couldn't be dismissed. I was trying to mold, and control Will, rather than fully accepting his carefree ways, and he deserved more.

After breaking up with Will, Steve and I met on several occasions that summer. He cooked a few breakfasts for me after my night shifts, and I prepared his catch of fresh fish for the three of us while he entertained my son, Michael. We got along well, like siblings; there was no romantic interest. At the end of summer, he returned to Indiana, and I started college to become a registered nurse.

A seemingly insignificant moment became a defining moment that summer. I stepped away from a land mine and into the first of four heal-ing stages. Across time and distance, our pen pal relationship flourished. In our written exchanges, I learned to trust him with my wounds and to trust myself and others in the face of significant challenges.

Woundedness is happening at epidemic levels all around us. In the US, one in five people suffer from mental health challenges, and one in eight people worldwide.[1] Our country is wounded: we have alarming suicide, anxiety, depression, and addiction rates. Perhaps you, like me, have firsthand experiences of woundedness, either personally or within your family or community. We are all injured in diverse ways at various times in our lives; it is a universal experience. Like the ebb and flow of water at the river's edge, large and small injuries come and go, frequently and often without our awareness, from seemingly insignificant hurt feelings to deep suffering. Some injuries are physical, others psychological, involving thoughts and feelings that originate in our minds, and some are a combination of the two. Feelings, often referred to as emotions, symbolically originate in the heart. As injuries occur, we suffer, sometimes down to the essence of our purpose for being, what I refer to as the soul, and lose all motivation to live.

I've written this memoir to inspire and encourage others on complex journeys by sharing my personal and professional nursing experiences of woundedness and healing. I invite you to discover the four stages of wound healing, the four As of **Nature's Natural Cycle of Emotional and Spiritual Healing,** and "**Recurring Resilience Practices** that promote well-being. I've formatted the book into four parts; each is a metaphor for one of the four stages of wound healing: hemostasis, inflammation, proliferation, and maturation.[2] The first reflects the process of survival; Part Two covers the painful process of defending and defeating. Part Three's focus is on rapid growth and repair of what is lost. Part Four describes remodeling as a process to improve form, function, and strength. Each part serves as a lens for viewing our spiritual and emotional healing as it relates to holistic healing of the mind, body, and spirit. Each stage builds upon the earlier stages. As you follow along on my healing journey, I hope that my story inspires you to recognize woundedness and or to make the changes in your own life that promote emotional healing across the four stages.

PART ONE

BLEEDING

HEMOSTASIS

Immediately following an injury to tissue, blood vessels constrict, and special cells aggregate to form a clot to prevent further bleeding and create a matrix for additional healing cells to collect. This process occurs in internal tissues where it is less evident, as well as externally, where bleeding is more evident.

1972 Michael and Me

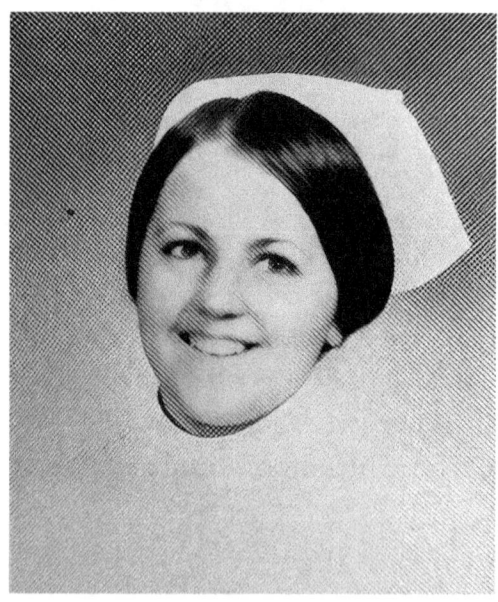

LPN School 1974

CHAPTER ONE

SURVIVAL INSTINCT

1970s, Duluth, Minnesota

I was used to planning and organizing my life as the oldest child of parents who lived in the moment and seldom planned to prevent problems. In fifth grade, I washed dishes in the cafeteria for free hot lunches. I used babysitting money to take the city bus downtown and shop for my own clothes. My parents depended on me from an early age to care for my three siblings. Ten-year-old Lee was my stepfather Don's favorite. She looked like Mom: dark hair and eyes with an olive complexion. We didn't look like sisters. I had blue eyes and bleached blond hair. Mom got me started on "Summer Blond" lightener in the sixth grade to cover my dirty blond. Lee had perfect teeth; mine were crooked, barely fitting in my small mouth with an underdeveloped upper jaw. She was shy and didn't talk back like I did. Paul was only a year younger than Lee, but his unusual short stature made him look half her age. Mom went back to work waitressing when my youngest brother Vincent was ten days old. I watched them from after school until after midnight, when my parents returned, often very drunk.

After years of being let down and broken promises, I learned to be independent and not to depend on others, especially if they were drinking. I was programmed to interpret the slurred speech, change in voice cues, or the way they walked, predicting when I needed to step in and compensate for their limitations. Just the scent of alcohol put me on high alert. If Mom was drunk, I kept her away from Dad. Booze made her brave and mouthy, which triggered fights that lasted through the night. The frequent moves, changes in schools, and then the added pressure of Vincent's birth added to an already stormy home life. They triggered greater resentment, mistrust, and an unhealthy cynicism toward my family.

Fred and I started dating exclusively just a few months after meeting at the roller-skating rink. He was sixteen and I was thirteen. I relied on him for comfort, acceptance, and transportation. My family moved six times in the first year of our relationship. He brought me home from West Junior High to the hotel that my family and I lived in in West Duluth when I started eighth grade, and to the trailer park behind Target when I transferred to Washington Junior High that same year. I believed he cared for me more than my family, and I was grateful to have him in my life. After ten months of sneaking out to see him against my parents' wishes, I got pregnant.

I hid the pregnancy from my parents until I was ready to activate my escape plan. My best friend, who'd also gotten pregnant in high school, helped me. She connected me with Mandy, a social worker from the welfare department near the Cascade Hotel, where my family and I were living. We shared a one-bedroom kitchenette, where my siblings and I all slept on a sofa bed. One month after confirming my pregnancy, my family moved from the hotel to a poorly furnished two-bedroom rental. Vincent didn't have a crib, and I carried a lamp from room to room as there were no ceiling lights.

I vividly recall the day I left home. It was a warm sunny day. Mandy came to the front door at about 10:00 a.m. Mom was in her bathrobe with a cigarette in her hand. As usual, she was reluctant to answer the door and appeared annoyed at the disruption. "What do you want?" she impatiently inquired.

After Mandy introduced herself, Mom mumbled something in her monotone voice and invited her in, pointing to the lime green sofa. Before their conversation continued, I ran upstairs on my tiptoes to avoid waking my stepfather, Don, and grabbed two prefilled paper grocery bags with all my belongings. I slowly crept down the stairs, listening as Mandy told Mom I was pregnant and moving out. I don't recall saying goodbye or even looking at Mom as I sheepishly walked out the front door, leaving the screen door to slam shut. Without looking back, I ran down the concrete steps and waited for Mandy. We drove a short distance to Hillcrest House, where I lived and attended school until ninth grade spring break.

On that memorable August day at my parents' house, I knew I had to escape, for my and the baby's safety. My alcoholic Stepfather, Don, had become increasingly unpredictable, argumentative, and physically abusive towards Mom and me since Vince had been born four months earlier. I hadn't thought about the burden Lee would bear in my absence, taking care of an infant and Paul. I was too overwhelmed and ashamed to consider their needs over mine at the time. Lee and I were never close after I left.

THE HOME FOR UNWED MOTHERS

The predictability, safety, and comfort at Hillcrest House were a relief from the constant chaos at home. It shielded me from verbal assaults and threats that were directed at me and my mom and helped me avoid sleep deprivation, as Don often woke me in the middle of the night to cook for him. I had time to myself, to think about my future without any other responsibilities. It didn't, however, shield me from conflict and pressure from well-meaning adults. In the safety of its walls, I would decide the fate of my unborn child.

Everyone had an opinion about what I should do with the baby. My plan, like most of us girls, was to place the baby for adoption. Mom was against adoption, probably because of her experience living in an orphanage as a child and then being pressured to place me for adoption when she got pregnant at seventeen. Fred's parents also wanted us to keep the baby, but they avoided the topic to avoid conflict.

My Grandma Betty was for adoption; she wanted to protect me from the hardships Mom had faced. I broke the news to her over lunch at the Captain's Table, across from the Radisson Hotel, where she waitressed at The Top of the Harbor. She arrived, still in her uniform, a dress fashioned after a sailor's uniform with a blue skirt, white bodice, and blue striped collar trimmed with a red scarf. Her almost blonde hair was nicely styled with stiff hairspray. I got a whiff of her familiar scent, White Shoulders perfume, as I seated myself across from her. Not ready to look her in the face, I stared at her hands, dreading the conversation to come. Her nails were neatly manicured, painted to hide yellow nicotine stains. She wore two rings: a wedding ring from her third husband and a gold ring with a black onyx stone from her deceased second husband. Her first husband was my grandfather, Frank.

"Grandma, I'm pregnant," I blurted out.

Before replying, she looked around to see if anyone had heard me. Then she moved her chair closer and whispered. "Oh no! Debbie, I'm so sorry to hear this. You want to finish school and be a nurse. You can't have a baby. You need help; someone who will help you put the baby up for adoption." She knew me well and supported my decision.

Even Don, my stepdad, had a plan for me. He had arranged, through the housemother, to take me to lunch. Riding across the bridge to Wisconsin, I wondered why he would be taking me to a fancy restaurant. We had never been on an outing together, except when I helped him at work. As we entered the dining room, he went straight to the bar and said, "Bring me a brandy Manhattan, we'll be by the window."

After being seated, he lit a cigarette and placed an order for burgers and fries with the waitress. When she left the table, he leaned toward me and said: "I know people who will pay a lot of money for this baby. They will pay to adopt your baby."

I was horrified by his suggestion. My pastor and Mandy would help me decide who would adopt the baby, not strangers. That day was frozen in time for me. I felt betrayed and manipulated. My heart had started to warm up to him, hoping this gesture would be the first of more to come. I had let my guard down, believing he really did care about me. I regained my composure and relaxed as reality set in. Nothing had changed. I felt pulled from all sides, yet firm in my decision. I wanted a better life for the baby than I could provide.

Hillcrest House was a five-story brick building built in the early 1900s. It looked like a mansion to me. It had beautifully carved dark woodwork, velvet drapes, and lots of old floral wallpaper. The visitors' room had a sunlit window with lace curtains and formal furniture. A sign-in book sat on a table in the front foyer. The lounge was on the top floor facing the lake. It had several faded overstuffed sofas, a TV, a wooden table with mismatched chairs, and a phone booth. It was the only place where girls could smoke in the building and make personal phone calls. It was also where we shared stories about the delivery room, as well as hopes and dreams for our babies. Overflowing ashtrays, pizza boxes, and food wrappers littered the room until Saturday, which was cleaning day.

My room was on the third floor, two doors down from a large, shared bathroom. It had an iron radiator for heat beneath the windows, linoleum floors, and soaring ceilings. Classrooms were in the walk-out basement, where I was the youngest in the home.

I had time to myself to think about my future without any other responsibilities. My free time was spent with Fred and his parents. His mom reminded me of Grandma Betty and my Sunday School teachers, and his dad treated me like his own daughter.

All of us girls at Hillcrest House looked out for each other, shared in completing assigned chores, and ate together. We attended classes in the morning, followed by lunch in the dining room. After lunch, we gathered in the visitors' room for group time led by Tip. She was a beloved friend to all of us. It was years before I discovered she was a paid social worker. Group time with Tip was when we got to know each other, sharing our struggles and concerns. We talked about everything from pregnancy and childbirth to family dynamics, fathers of our babies, school, and ultimately our plans after delivery. The girls were at various stages of pregnancy or had recently delivered and were in the process of making new living arrangements. This was the first home I'd lived in where I felt comfortable and safe.

The house staff and eight to ten girls ate meals together in a family-style setting. Mrs. Lyndon, the cook, was my favorite staff person. She spoke with a heavy German accent, and she was always talkative and friendly. Her generous spirit was appreciated by the girls and anyone else who stopped in her kitchen. She was motherly toward us in a kind and nourishing way. Her gray hair was contained under a net, and a full-length white apron covered her cotton print dress, which barely held her bosom. I spent hours listening to her tell stories of girls who had come and gone as she prepared meals, punched bread dough, and rolled pie crust.

January 1972, Hospital Elevator

Looking outward from inside the hospital elevator toward the newborn nursery viewing windows is another moment frozen in time that I'll never forget. As the elevator doors closed, I watched my firstborn child fade from view, closing the door to that chapter of my life. I wasn't sure if I'd ever recover. It was unlike me to admit I couldn't do something. I knew it wasn't a lack of ability to love and care for him;

it was out of a need to protect him from my painful world, a world of poverty, alcoholism, and living day by day without the assurance of future needs being met. I wanted more for him. At that moment, I longed for another baby someday, one that I would be able to keep, who would help me bear his loss. As the doors closed, I felt like life was being squeezed from me. I was glad to be leaving after five days feeling ignored, disrespected, and humiliated.

Fred and I exited the elevator and the front entrance. It was minus six degrees outside, with snow flurries. The snow crunched under our boots as we hurriedly reached his 1966 Plymouth. I was glad to escape the control and oversight of the hospital, as I was used to being independent in caring for myself. I felt ignored and disrespected by the nurses. I read that breast milk contains colostrum, something that boosts the baby's immunity. I wanted to provide that for the baby, but I was given an injection to dry up my breast milk before I left the delivery table. I also read that cuddling was good for the baby. I had to argue with the nurses and beg them to let me hold him. They said it was for my own good since I was giving him up. Who were they to judge? I did hold him, every chance I could, for the five days I was there. Each time I held him, knowing it was temporary, I sang, I cried, and I prayed for God's protection and the best possible parents for him.

Fred and I rode in silence to the Hillcrest House, both of us mentally exhausted. He dropped me off at the front door and left for home. I signed myself in and went straight to my room, passing guests in the visitors' room. I didn't feel like talking to anyone. As I climbed the three flights to my room, I felt burning around the stitches holding torn tissue together between my legs, and a heaviness in my heart. I comforted myself under the weight of blankets and drifted off to sleep. An hour later, someone knocked on my door to tell me I had a phone call. I moved slowly as I approached the phone booth, trying to limit movements that tugged the stitches between my legs. It was Fred calling to say, "My parents don't want us to give up the baby. They'll help so you don't have to give him up."

I hadn't expected the call, but I wasn't surprised. His parents had seen the baby at the hospital, and I sensed their discomfort with my decision. The phone call was awkward as he dismantled my defenses for choosing adoption and challenged my faith and trust in him and his family. They had been kind to me, offering warmth and acceptance without judgment. Since I craved acceptance, my default was to give in to others' requests, often against my better judgment. Now, I was caught off guard. The call concluded with the agreement that we would return to the hospital in the morning to pick up our son.

I spent the night in my room, embracing my new role as Michael's mom and devising a plan to finish school and to support us. I promised myself I'd become the mother my mother was unable to be, and this baby would know he was loved, cared for, and safe. I knew this would be impossible without help, so I prayed. As I spoke to God, I began to feel a sense of relief and comfort. The words from Sunday school songs like "Jesus Loves Me" and "Trust and Obey" played in my head. Slowly, the tears stopped flowing, my clenched jaw relaxed, and hope soothed my soul, overshadowing my earlier raw feelings of despair and desperation. I was no longer under the blankets, crying. Instead, I was wide awake and took the first step as Michael's mom. I emptied the bottom drawer of the bedside stand, which held trinkets, mementos, letters, and cards —symbols of my childhood. All were discarded into the trash. My childhood was now behind me, and in its place was a new life as Michael's mom. I wasn't sure how I would care for him, but I knew I was not alone, and God would help me.

By morning, I had convinced myself everything would be okay. However, I wasn't confident I'd ever marry Fred. Consequently, I'd planned life as a single mom, giving up control and accepting help from Fred and his family. I called Mandy to let her know the new plan.

Next, I notified the house mother. She helped me search the attic for a crib. Together, we assembled an ancient white metal crib and set it up in my room in time for me to meet Fred out front for the ride back to the hospital.

Stepping into the hospital elevator, I no longer felt the overwhelming feeling of loss and sadness I had experienced the day before. "I'm here to take my son home," I reported to the clerk at the nurse's station.

The earlier feelings of being repressed and ignored by the nurses evaporated into joy. I gave no thought to the family who expected to take him home that day; the family who would lose hope of becoming his adopted parents. Instead, my thoughts were on getting to Target ahead of the predicted snowstorm to buy baby supplies. Fred arrived with a baby sleeper and a handmade quilt to wrap baby Michael in, which made me wonder if this was Fred's mother's plan all along.

SCHOOL NURSES OFFICE, APRIL 1972

I was unexpectedly called to the nurse's office by Miss Bujold, the school nurse, on my second day back at Washington Junior High. She was middle-aged, dressed in a beige sweater dress belted at the waist with a colorful scarf draped around her shoulders, and a loose beige bun crowning her head. As I entered her office, her red-painted lips turned into a smile as she handed me a package and peered into my face, saying, "I hope everything is well with you and your baby."

There was a rattle, and a bottle of Avon cologne wrapped in pink and blue tissue paper. Her warmth and lack of judgment caught me off guard. "I see you are one credit short of graduating from ninth grade," she said, peering through her glasses that had slid down her nose, followed by, "I think I can help you if you're willing to help me."

I knew I wouldn't proceed to high school without going to summer school, so her comment intrigued me. She invited me to work in her office during my study hall for one unit of independent study, checking students in and taking their temperature. Her offer allowed me to take a high school English class in the summer and start tenth grade in the fall. I will never forget her kindness and consideration.

EMANCIPATION, 1973

In the fall of 1973, I started my senior year after completing both the tenth and eleventh grade course requirements the previous year. Michael and I lived with my parents until it was no longer bearable, and Mandy, my social worker, found us an emergency foster home placement. They were a lovely family with five children and had a positive experience with another foster daughter with a baby, and so they warmly welcomed Michael and me into their home. Since we agreed that arranging for daycare was my responsibility, I walked Michael to a licensed home daycare near the foster home and caught the city bus to school. By week two, I lost confidence in the daycare mom. When I picked Michael up, half of his food and milk were still in the diaper bag, and his diapers were always soaked. I decided to stop taking Michael there, especially when I discovered that his caregiver was attending Parents Anonymous, a support group for parents with a history of child abuse. I couldn't risk Michael becoming a victim of abuse, so I explained the situation to Fred and his parents. The next day, Fred started taking me to school and leaving Michael with his dad for the day while he worked. This continued until we got married.

With permission from the court, I was married during my senior year. I was sixteen. Two months earlier, I broke my ankle in a sledding accident and was placed in a non-weight-bearing cast with crutches. Not even my broken leg could stop the wedding plans. I was eager to get out from under my parents' roof after being back home with them for four months following my foster mom's emergency surgery.

Our reception was an inexpensive family affair at a hotel near the restaurant dad worked at. My in-laws donated cash for the food, and Don prepared it. Fifty people came to the reception, including my birth father, Lyle, and his family, whom I'd recently met.

I met my birth father's family the month before the wedding at a shower hosted by an auntie. The resemblance between me and my aunts was striking; we shared a similar underdeveloped upper jaw. The physical resemblance and their genuine warmth attracted me like a magnet to them. Discovering five new half-siblings and my grandparents, Helen and Lyle, brought the joy of a newfound sense of belonging into my life; something I had always craved.

REFLECTIONS

In the first stage of wound healing, the body goes into survival mode, minimizing the loss of blood to preserve life. Feeling afraid and unsafe, that's exactly what I did. I mentally went into survival mode. However, having access to accurate information and resources about being pregnant was essential for thriving, as essential as blood is to life for surviving. Information from my case worker, teachers, and Tip, the group leader, helped me in forming reality-based perceptions of physical and emotional behaviors in myself and others. Slowly, I began to trust myself, the team at the maternity home, Fred's family, and my Creator, relinquishing the need to be in control of everything. Although the experience was unfortunate, my emotional well-being, confidence, and ability to develop trusting relationships improved as my sense of safety increased.

CHAPTER TWO

CONTROLLING THE FLOW

The summer of 1974 was a happy time. The Vietnam War was winding down, Nixon resigned from office, sparing the country further harm and division, and I graduated from high school at seventeen, having become a wife and mother. I looked forward to starting the licensed practical nursing (LPN) program in September. Fred and I were no longer living with his parents. We had a three-bedroom house that his parents helped us buy for $14,000. They paid $1,000 down payment and arranged for us to buy it with a fifteen-year loan on a contract for deed for $140 a month. Fred was working night shifts at a decal factory, and I was cashiering in the evenings at Shopper City–the same Shopper City that Steve would work at as security years later, which I mentioned in the introduction. Life was going well for us despite the recession, with a 12 percent inflation rate and the highest unemployment rate in thirty-five years, steady at fifteen percent.

But then on a sweltering summer night, my world crashed in on me, leaving me confused, angry, and broken-hearted. I arrived home from work to an empty house. Fred was working the night shift, and Michael was at my in-laws' for the night. I was about to go to bed when I got a phone call from Gary, one of Fred's friends.

"Do you know where Fred is?"

"Yeah, he's at work. Why do you want to know?"

"Debbie, he's not at work, he's at my place and... and he's with someone."

I paused, wondering if this was a joke. "Really, Deb, I'm sorry. I just thought you should know."

And then the phone went dead. I was so angry that I began shaking. I wondered if this had anything to do with the warning notice I had found in his jeans when I was washing clothes. The note on official work stationery said he would be placed on suspension if he were reckless at work again. My heart sank as I read it, but I chose to ignore it, hoping he'd take the warning seriously. It felt like a note from the principal's office, and my kid was in trouble. I was concerned because I didn't want a marriage like my mom's; to be powerless and accept irresponsible behavior. I had to be able to trust Fred, and lately, I hadn't. I wondered, should I ignore the phone call and pretend I didn't know, like I did with the warning note?

I was so upset that I couldn't ignore the call, nor could I sleep, so I walked to Gary's place to check on Fred. Back in high school, Gary's place was known as a party place. When Fred and I first met, that's where we hung out after school. I peeked in the front door, heard loud music, and saw Fred off in the distance with a girl I didn't recognize. They were making out. I slowly shut the door and as tears welled up in my eyes and ran toward the sidewalk. Grandma lived nearby, so I headed to her place. She was my confidant and a source of comfort, always a good listener, and I trusted her advice. As I got closer to her place, I imagined myself knocking at her door and realized Al, her new husband, would probably answer. At that moment, for the first time ever, I felt like an outsider in my grandma's life, and I realized what an imposition I would be showing up in the middle of the night. I didn't want to be a burden. She'd been through enough, losing her mom, daughter, and second husband within a few years. Grandma and Al made a great couple. I no longer fit in her life like before. Saddened by the thought, I continued walking.

I reached the church where Fred and I were married, recalling the day. Our honeymoon ended when we moved out of his parents' house and into our own place. That's when the party lifestyle began. I stopped trusting Fred to watch Michael when I found Michael in our closet sucking on a bong like an experienced stoner. We constantly argued over his drinking, the parties, and money. And more recently, we had argued about my weight gain. I was up twenty pounds. I couldn't accept the way things were going, and now the call tonight confirmed my suspicions: we were headed toward divorce. My eyes watered so much I could hardly see. I was torn between keeping a vow and moving on without him. The future was as blurry as my vision under the glow of the streetlight.

I headed toward Mom and Dad's apartment. Mom would be off work soon, and Dad would be picking her up since he was now on disability for anxiety neurosis. As I approached their apartment, I could hear Mom in my head say, "Debra, you're so emotional; if you'd lose weight, everything would be fine."

She overlooked problems, or just denied them, and she'd expect me to do the same, because divorce was not an option in her Catholic world. A block from Mom's, I realized I was on my own and alone. The next move was mine to make alone.

I didn't want to go home, so I kept walking. I walked four more miles to the end of the Park Point bus line, where Mom used to take us swimming. I sat at a picnic table until pink, orange, and yellow lights peeked through the morning sky, announcing a new day.

Four hours later, I arrived home, and the house was empty. With each step I took that night, on my twenty-mile journey into reality, my thoughts and feelings brought me closer to a decision. Our relationship was over. In my anger, rage, and pain, I locked the doors and put a note on the screen that said, "I know where you were last night. We're done."

And then, after I tossed his clothes out the bedroom window, I went to bed, exhausted.

By the end of summer, I filed for divorce and became eligible for unexpected resources to fuel my desire and passion to complete an LPN program in a vocational trade school. Mandy, my old social worker, helped me secure assistance for childcare, food stamps, and medical care through the state of Minnesota, Aid to Families with Dependent Children, also known as "welfare." I swallowed my pride and accepted the help, believing someday I would be able to give back.

Mandy enrolled me in the WIN program, a state-funded work incentive program designed to decrease dependence on government help through job training. According to her, the hardest part of getting into the WIN program was to first getting accepted into a training program, like the LPN program I was starting.

Fred's dad drove me to classes and took care of Michael for the first six weeks of nurse training. I was eager to break the ties of dependence on him and found a nearby licensed home day care recommended by a friend. By Christmas, Michael was potty-trained and enjoying his friends at daycare.

I found a carpool with three of my classmates from high school to help with transportation. We paid Heather $5 a week to drive us to and from school and the hospital. Monday morning, my carpool mates shared their weekend activities, which I had not participated in. I was still working weekends as a grocery clerk and was busy after work with Michael. I envied their freedom and camaraderie outside of school. I felt like an invisible outsider on Monday mornings.

LPN classes were held on campus in the classroom and lab for the first three months. The remaining seven months were spent at the hospital from 7:00 a.m. to 3:30 p.m. Starting in our first week, Mrs. Claveau, a short, broad nurse with short grey hair, made it clear that missing school or clinic time was not an option. We were advised to drop the program if we needed to take any time off during the school year. I missed a lot of school growing up, either from helping Mom or from frequent ear infections. Now I was determined to not miss any school and to succeed in the LPN program.

Our first lesson was about empathy, caring, and compassion; the foundation of the nursing profession. I didn't know what empathy meant, but recognized it when I heard the definition. Empathy is what Grandma Betty taught me by example. I was fortunate to begin my nursing training in this vocational education program, as it prepared me for college and the RN program. Each week, we reviewed one of the body's organ systems, focusing on the anatomy, basic physiology, normal function, diseases, and usual treatments for each of the systems. Communication skills, math, medication administration, and care of the bedridden patient were taught using films and demonstrations by the lab instructors.

I thrived in the program. It served as an outlet for my constant curiosity, a focus outside of myself and my sadness, and provided the order and predictability I craved. For the first time in my life, I followed a plan with clear goals and guidance. I had policies, procedures, and a well-thought-out patient care plan developed by the registered nurses. I wasn't left to figure things out on my own. The physical environment was also well thought out, with separation between the clean and dirty utility rooms and a place for recording and storing patient progress records: the chartroom. My days were full. There was no room for drama. I was on a mission to become a nurse and provide for Michael and me.

In December, I quit my cashier job in order to start clinical days at the hospital. Our class was divided into cohort groups of five to seven students, who stayed together throughout the program. This provided opportunities to get to know and learn from each other during our hospital experiences. Hospital shifts concluded with a debriefing session facilitated by an instructor to promote learning, camaraderie, and team-building skills. Each group rotated through pediatrics, medical, surgical, obstetrics and gynecology, cardiology, and psychiatric units between two local hospitals.

My last rotation was in the psychiatric unit where street clothes, not uniforms, were the norm. I no longer had to wear the size fourteen pin-striped uniform I was drowning in since losing twenty pounds. By graduation, my divorce was final. I lost both my heavy heart and my excess weight while gaining self-acceptance and confidence.

One week before my eighteenth birthday, my divorce was finalized. I struggled with conflicting emotions. My sadness was in knowing we would never be the family I had hoped for, and the pain was rooted in failure to honor a sacred vow. The truth was that we were both immature and unprepared for the demands of marriage and parenthood, and the longer we delayed the inevitable, the more difficult it would become.

The prospect of a new beginning was appealing. No more trying to be the good wife married to Peter Pan. By the end of May, an unexpected sense of joy settled in, which unexpectedly led to feeling guilty for being happy. My happiness seemed to be the same kind of happiness I experienced when I married into Fred's family. They had filled my craving for a trusting, compassionate, and safe home. I cared deeply for his parents, but I no longer trusted him. Rather, I trusted my gut feelings and let go.

As I stepped into the hospital elevator, on my last week of school, I was surprised to see Steve. He looked just like I remembered him from high school: no evidence of facial hair, straight auburn hair swept across his forehead, and perfect teeth. My first memories of him were in the second grade, when he climbed aboard the school bus. He was friendly and adorable, always smiling. He had a thick hillbilly drawl, so strong I could barely understand him, and he wore a bow tie and fedora-style hat.

In sixth-grade Sunday school, Steve and I held hands behind our backs while sitting next to each other in a circle, thinking no one noticed. On a winter hayride with the youth group, he lent me his hat and wrapped his arms around my shoulders, hoping I'd stop shivering. That had been during mom's pregnancy when I didn't have to babysit. I also recall that it was during a church softball game when Steve suggested I break up with Fred before I ended up pregnant. Steve's prediction was sadly too late; the next time I saw him in church, I was seven months pregnant with Michael.

Prior to this hospital meeting, my last memory of Steve was an evening in the school library when I was taking Civics as an independent study, two months before my wedding. He was passing through after theater practice on his way home. We had no difficulty picking up where our last conversations had ended. We knew of each other's hardships, dealing with alcoholism in our families and feelings of abandonment. At age five, his mother was unable to care for him and sent him to live with a cousin and her husband in Duluth.

Seeing Steve in the hospital elevator put me at ease. His gaze was engaging, and his voice gentle. In that brief encounter, he explained he worked in the laundry department and was leaving for college in September. We agreed to meet in the hospital cafeteria for lunch the next day. I told him about the divorce, and I shared pictures of Michael. Our cafeteria conversations were enjoyable and engaging, and I had no expectation of seeing him again.

Passing the State Board of Nursing Examination was the climax of the LPN program. The girls from the carpool and I drove two and a half hours south to the Twin Cities to take the exam. It was the farthest I had ever been from home. We all stayed overnight in a hotel and took the exam the next day. When I called Mom two months later to tell her I had passed, her reply surprised me. In her matter-of-fact, stoic voice, she said, "Of course you did; I had no doubt you'd pass."

At that moment, I realized that my mom had more confidence in me than I did in myself. I had distanced myself from her out of anger and felt as though she didn't understand me. When we were at odds, she'd say, "Debra, you're too emotional. We don't have to talk about problems. Why do you complicate everything and turn it into a problem? Everything's fine."

Despite our differences, she always believed in the best of me and did her best to avoid confrontations.

I was hired to work in the orthopedic department, where patients were often bedridden for many weeks at a time. Patients with total joint replacements stayed for a week or two, and others with complicated fractures requiring traction and long-term wound care frequently stayed for several months. I especially looked forward to evening care, when patients tethered to their beds in traction and splints were lifted by a team of assistants for basic nursing and comfort care. We rubbed their backs and butts, checked for pressure sores, applied lotion, refreshed their bed linen, and offered them a bedpan. Oral care and weekly shampoo followed. Mutual trust and gratitude flowed between patients and the nurses and within the nursing team.

As an LPN, I was a member of a team led by an RN. As a new nurse, I rotated between nights, evenings, and the day shift. I hired "Grandma Rose," a neighbor, to care for Michael when I worked evening and night shifts. I wanted him to have the security of a routine, sleeping in his own bed at night, not his grandparents'. Rose remained with us until my grandfather moved in the following year.

Dorothy Rust, RN, was my team leader on the 3:00 to 11:00 p.m. shift. She was an ex-Navy nurse in her late fifties, thin and wiry with short auburn hair, wire-rimmed glasses, and thin, orange-painted lips. She had an amazing energy level, a cheerful outlook, and was a joy to be around. Dorothy was a mentor, a role model, and a frequent volunteer in her church and community. I admired her.

One evening at the end of shift report, Dorothy suggested I consider returning to school to become a registered nurse, the goal I had abandoned for practical reasons. It still seemed impractical, but the thought of realizing my dream and becoming like Dorothy and the other RNs was tempting. I weighed the pros and cons of going back to school and dedicated this subject to my daily prayers, asking for God's wisdom and direction. I shared my prayer request with the ladies from my neighborhood church.

Realizing a Dream

The week following my talk with Dorothy, Mom called to tell me she had met, on my behalf, with the admissions office at the College of Saint Scholastica (CSS) to see if my Native American background would qualify me for tuition assistance. According to Mom, I could apply for the fall semester of 1976 now and attend the only local four-year nursing program. However, I was not eligible for scholarships for Native Americans, and the annual tuition was out of my reach: $5,000 a year. Each day I worked with RNs, I became more convinced of my potential to become an RN and hopeful that a means to attend school would surface. After prayerful consideration, I believed my future as an RN was in God's hands, but I needed to act, too. Deciding to apply for college admission and financial aid was a step of faith nurtured in prayer. I found comfort in prayer and the belief of a higher power that cared about me and about my well-being, who offered guidance, hope, and relief from burdens as well as comfort in times of uncertainty, grief, and sadness. I had been the recipient of these gifts since learning of them in Sunday school and church. The practice of prayer, meditation, and the study of the Bible had connected me with God; however, I had to do my part and complete the college application.

The College of Saint Scholastica (CSS) financial aid package helped me achieve my dream of becoming an RN. I qualified for student loans as well as Benedictine College grants and scholarships. The Federal Nurse Traineeship Act provided funds to the college, and the college used the funds to provide grants to nursing students. I had ten years to pay back a total of $10,000 in student loans and, if I worked in a low-income community, there was a possibility of partial loan forgiveness.

REFLECTIONS

The key to minimizing harm from our physical wounds lies in part in our ability to recognize and respond quickly to prevent fatal blood loss and life-threatening infections (part of the survival mode). I needed to act quickly before my pregnancy was obvious if I wanted to control my circumstances. Honest self-reflection, investigating my feelings, helped me to recognize that I needed to seek help outside of my family. I believed I was loved, and they were trying their best, but I couldn't rely on them. Accepting help from Fred's family, friends, and professional services minimized the risk of harm to Michael and me. I've come to recognize social support systems and services as necessary safety nets that minimize harm to individuals and their families, the backbone of our cultures and societies. The reciprocal act of giving and receiving help minimized my risk for lifelong eroding self-esteem, regret, and resentment. Honest self-reflection informed my decisions, which helped me avoid costly mistakes. On an unconscious level, seeing Steve at Shopper City (in the introduction) was the catalyst that revealed my tendency to form unhealthy relationships and a desire to break free from them.

CHAPTER THREE

TARGETING RESPONSES

In the winter of 1977, I was admitted to the hospital with a life-threatening infection. Full-time school and weekend shifts distracted me from the life-threatening infection brewing in my pelvis over several weeks. My lack of sleep and poor eating habits caught up with me, depleting my immunity. A war was being fought inside of me, and I could no longer ignore it.

Doubled over in pain, I was no longer able to stand up straight, and Kathy, my partner in the cadaver lab, noticed. "Deb, I really think you should see your doctor."

Hesitantly, I left for my doctor's office. I checked in at the reception desk, barely able to stand, and was promptly brought to an exam room. After the lab results came back, I was sent to the emergency room, where an ultrasound revealed large pockets of pus in both Fallopian tubes. This prompted an admission to the hospital to prevent the tubes from bursting and spreading infection throughout my abdomen. My infection was most likely related to a sexually transmitted disease (STD), which gained access to my uterus from the string on the Intrauterine Device (IUD) I used for contraception. The IUD served as a source for bacteria to access my uterus. By the time I got to my hospital room, I was shaking uncontrollably. My temperature was 104 degrees. Intravenous antibiotics were started. I wasn't allowed to eat, as surgery was scheduled for the morning. My pastor was notified of my admission. He came and prayed with me.

A repeat ultrasound in the morning showed the abscesses were shrinking, so surgery was cancelled. I stayed in the hospital receiving IV antibiotics for four days until my temperature was normal for twenty-four hours. I missed two days of classes; Kathy took notes for me.

My nursing supervisor checked in to say hi. I was embarrassed to see her, as I didn't want her to know I was being treated for a sexually transmitted infection. There was no hiding it. I didn't want or need her judgment, for I had already swallowed the shame. I was grateful she didn't mention it.

Time off work allowed time for introspection and soul searching. I had no idea where my infection came from. It could have been from Fred during the summer, when in a moment of weakness, I gave in to his advances, or perhaps I had contracted it from Will or one of the guys I dated after him. I wasn't sure. However, I was sure of one thing: I couldn't expect sexual encounters to fill my need for love and affection. I needed to change my ways.

I sought the counsel of the campus priest. His words were kind and nonjudgmental, and his demeanor was caring. He had good advice. He said sometimes it's worse to give in to the weaknesses of the flesh and suffer the consequences than it is to stay strong and avoid those weaknesses. He was right. My indiscretions had unintended consequences, and they would haunt me for years to come.

SPRING, 1978

The discharge planner at the hospital informed me of Grandpa's upcoming discharge. Grandpa Frank had a large presence in my life. He was 5'8" and 250 pounds, with a round, balding head, a large abdomen, and a loud voice. He wore his signature uniform, rotating between green and gray docker pants and a matching button-down work shirt, topped off with a matching work hat, a lightweight zip-up jacket, and sturdy Redwing work boots. He was always clean-shaven and smelled like soap. He was my Godfather and a member of the longshoremen's union. He supervised the loading of ships with general cargo and grain. Years of shoveling grain had contributed to his dry cough and chronic bronchitis. He described himself as a man's man and was not afraid to put a shovel in his hand.

During my weekend shift, I visited Grandpa during my dinner break. He had been hospitalized in intensive care for complications from bronchitis and binge drinking. He was an alcoholic and was going to be discharged the next day. According to Grandma, he never drank when they were married, but his obsessive-compulsive disorder was more than she could manage, and she wanted to shield her children from his constant anxious state.

She divorced him in 1949, but Grandpa's heart remained married until he died. After the divorce, he lived a semi-monastic lifestyle following the teachings of Jesus, "the guy who had nothing except the nightgown on his back," as Grandpa would say. His entire earthly possessions fit in a small duffel bag, which he carted in his car from hotels to motels.

Fearing a relapse, I suggested he move in with me. I wanted to help him recover and get back into his routine with Alcoholics Anonymous. The timing was great, as my sister Lee had recently moved out of my spare bedroom. It was important to be there for him, as he had been for me over the years. He was a mentor to me; he taught Bible stories, took me to church, and practiced what he preached when the opportunity presented itself.

Without hesitation, Grandpa agreed to move in with Michael and me. The next day, I drove him to the Seaway Hotel to check out of his room and pick up his car. He agreed to give me $90 a month, which helped both of us. It didn't take him long to form an attachment to Michael. I enjoyed his company and accepted his rigid obsessions, compulsions, and poor manners. He prided himself on being intelligent, yet he had no idea how rude he was when things didn't go the way he wanted. I learned how to avoid triggering him into a fit of anger or anxiousness by never interrupting him as he went down his checklist, nor could I enter his bedroom or bathroom, even to do something nice for him. He was religious about attending daily communion and weekly AA meetings.

After Grandpa's income taxes were filed, he usually left for warmer weather until the shipping season reopened. He stayed in Duluth the first winter of living with me. This gave us an opportunity to adjust to each other. He resumed work in the spring, with two years to go before retirement, when he'd cash in on his union pension. He lived with me until 1980, when, after graduation, I moved.

THE ULTIMATUM

I didn't see it coming. I guess I was naïve, or I just couldn't believe Steve could ever be interested in me romantically. I guess I should have suspected it; turns out he had feelings for me. It was 1978 when he drove to Duluth over spring break and asked if he could stay with me. I let him sleep on my sofa bed, and during the day, while I was at work, he cleaned my house, which offended me. I was dating another guy whom I met on a blind date and had plans with him on my weekend off. If my house guest was upset, he didn't show it. On a side note, my Grandpa Frank took a liking to Steve. He judged my dates by their footwear. He didn't like the guy I was dating who wore penny loafers, but he liked Steve's sensible work boots.

The following summer, Steve took a job as a deckhand on a US Steel laker, transporting iron ore on the Great Lakes. He invited Michael and me to visit him and take a tour of the ship when it docked in Two Harbors. Traveling thirty miles to see him was the farthest I'd ever driven from home. Michael and I enjoyed our visit. I thanked him for including us and headed home.

In my mind, I wasn't good enough to be Steve's girlfriend, so I never entertained the idea. Or maybe it was that I thought he was too good for me. I never hid my shame around him; he knew my secrets, past mistakes, and vulnerabilities. When I wrote to him about my ambivalence about getting divorced, his kind and compassionate response caught me off guard.

"Deb, I believe our God is a loving and forgiving God who wants you to be happy, and you were still a child when you married Fred and shouldn't be held responsible for the mistakes of a child."

He suggested I ask God for forgiveness and move on with my life.

In September of 1978, Steve wrote to tell me we could no longer be friends. He was giving me an ultimatum: I had to choose him as my only boyfriend or lose our friendship. It was too painful for him to be overlooked. He confessed he had been in love with me since the sixth grade and the church hayride, and after all these years, he wanted to marry me. I was shocked, and yet the signs had been there all along.

In addition to being caught off guard about Steve's feelings for me, I was also astonished at his physical transformation over the summer, working on board the ship. With three months of heavy manual labor, unlimited kitchen access with meals cooked by US Steel's finest chef, Steve put on thirty pounds. He was no longer the skinny boy I knew. He had grown in maturity, both physically and emotionally, with a deeper understanding of himself and what he wanted.

In October, Steve announced he was going to be in Duluth for a few days, since he was helping his parents move back there. We agreed to meet while he was in town. On the day he was to arrive, I was restless and arranged a visit with Grandma Betty. As I entered her back door, the sweet and pungent smell of ginger, cloves, and cinnamon aroused my senses. Knowing I was coming over, Grandma had baked my favorite molasses cookies. We chatted over cookies and milk as I told Grandma about Steve, our history, and my plans to meet him later in the day. That is when I asked her, "Grandma, how did you know Al was the right person for you?"

Without a pause, she had a reply, "Oh, Debbie, it's simple. When it's no longer a question in your mind, it just makes sense; there's no doubt or questions about it."

I met Steve at the Country Kitchen near the mall. Upon seeing him, I abandoned any notion of studying for my biology exam that evening, and instead, I spent several hours fully disarmed and charmed while visiting him. I left with a new perspective of our relationship and decided we were an exclusive couple. There was no question about it: Steve was the right one for me. It seemed too good to be true. We made plans to see each other over Thanksgiving break in Indiana. Without realizing it, I had been elevating Steve on a pedestal since our Sunday school days. It was time for me to see myself through Steve's eyes, as an equal.

My first airplane flight was to see Steve in Indiana. He literally sold plasma to pay for half of my ticket. My best friend, Kay, drove me two hours to the airport. We saw an on-campus play the night I arrived. The next day, we shared Thanksgiving dinner with five of his seven sisters and their families. The four-hour drive along winding, narrow country roads lined in fall colors went by fast. We talked about our plans for the next year, and he told me about the family he was reunited with when he moved back to Indiana to attend college.

His sisters were especially happy to see him, and everyone was friendly to me. We stayed the night with his sister Peggy and returned to campus the next day. I marveled at their Southern accents and smiled at their teasing ways, which made me feel welcome and included.

Steve drove seventeen hours in a snowstorm to spend Christmas break with Michael and me. He stayed at his parents' new place. He proposed to me on Christmas Eve in front of my humble tree. He sold his new stereo to buy my engagement ring, and I bought him the *Dark Side of the Moon* album by Pink Floyd.

Our wedding was scheduled for August, allowing him time to find a job after graduation. Steve oversaw our honeymoon plans, and I took charge of the wedding and reception. It was a long winter, and to make it longer, Steve stayed on campus over spring break to work and pay off his tuition. We resumed letter writing, with increased passion between the lines. I looked forward to our weekly phone calls on Sundays, when the rates were lowest.

Prior to the wedding, the pastor from the church we attended in our youth provided premarital counseling. This included a personality inventory assessment of both of us. Our results were the same with one exception: I scored extremely high on the extrovert scale, and Steve scored the opposite; he was truly an introvert. Steve had been baptized by this same pastor at twelve and had performed my baptism when I was an infant. At the pastor's suggestion, I took part in a full-immersion baptism prior to the wedding. My faith in the 'church' was renewed by the pastor's acceptance and support of our wedding plans, which helped me shed the prior shame of divorce.

We were married on a hot August afternoon. I wore a long, ivory, cotton Gunny Sacks dress trimmed in lace, and my maid of honor, Kay, wore a long red and white gingham-checked sundress. We both carried long-stemmed red roses. Steve wore a tan polyester suit from JCPenney. His college roommate was our best man. Eight-year-old Michael was our ring bearer, and he came with his grandparents, my ex-in-laws.

We joyfully paraded down the aisle together to the tune of "Music Box Dancer" and accepted our heartfelt personalized vows to each other before being introduced as Mr. and Mrs. Steven and Debra

Palmer. I convinced the pastor to forgo the tradition of introducing me as Mrs. Steven Palmer. "Morning Has Broken" ushered us to the front of the church.

Thirty guests were in attendance. Don was not there. He was on a psychiatric disability from work and seldom left the house. Grandma and Al brought Mom and my siblings, since Mom didn't drive. Steve's dad (my cousin's husband) made the wedding cake and carefully transported it to the church basement. Grandma and other family members brought food and helped set up the reception.

Honeymoon

We gathered with friends in the bar of the hotel where we stayed on our wedding night. A live band was playing contemporary tunes. We danced to disco music and slowed the pace for "Evergreen" by Barbra Streisand, the last dance of the night.

We woke early to pack our rental car for our honeymoon: a fishing trip in the Boundary Waters Canoe Area. We returned three days early after running out of food. It wasn't until after our tent was set up that I asked where the food was. I figured he had planned the meals, and he thought I did. We got over that misunderstanding quickly, as Steve was sure we'd catch plenty of fish. We survived on wild blueberries, granola bars, and popcorn. Our attempts to catch fish, who seemed to be resting on the bottom of the deep glacier-made lakes, were fruitless.

Upon arriving back in Duluth, we checked into a hotel, showered, and left for the Pickwick Restaurant for a long overdue meal, paid for the meal with a gift certificate: our wedding gift from Mom. After lunch, we toured the nearby Glensheen Mansion and its massive grounds overlooking Lake Superior. At the tour's conclusion, while walking through the parking lot, I was overcome with abdominal pains; the same pains I had suffered for the past five years without warning or explanation. Reflecting on that moment in the parking lot, I wondered if my sudden sense of panic was triggered by the thought that my life was not mine alone anymore and I'd be sharing it with a man. Or perhaps the pain was triggered by the fear of losing my independence and control, or maybe all three.

THREE MONTHS LATER

Our family of three took a week off over Thanksgiving break to vacation in Florida. My aunt, a travel agent, convinced us to book an all-inclusive vacation for the two of us for $750. Michael was an extra $100. The trip included hotel, car rental, airfare, and complimentary tickets to Disney World, Sea World, and Busch Gardens. We charged the trip to my Montgomery Ward's credit card.

We left town in blizzard conditions and arrived in Orlando under sunny skies and light rain with temperatures in the seventies. The rain seemed to have scared away park visitors, as there were no long lines at Disney. The next day, we were entertained by the size and grace of Shamu the whale at SeaWorld. Our ride through Busch Gardens felt like an African safari. On our last day, we went deep-sea fishing and swam with dolphins on Sanibel Island. Driving back to the hotel, I marveled at the orange groves and palm trees along the highway and the warmth of the sun. This was a life-changing trip. For the first time ever, I contemplated leaving Duluth after graduation.

SENIOR YEAR OF NURSING SCHOOL

My senior year was the best year of my college experience. Steve was working at a residential treatment facility for troubled youth, and I was no longer on welfare. Instead of working as an LPN every weekend, I worked one or two weekends a month. Hospital rotations had been replaced with public health nursing in the community, and all of my elective courses were enjoyable. Our trip to Florida influenced Steve's decision to apply to law schools in areas with less inclement weather. He was accepted to Gonzaga Law School in Spokane, Washington.

During spring break, I flew to Spokane for a job interview and accepted a position in the intensive care unit (ICU). During my final quarter, I was busy preparing for the move. Steve took time off work to drive with his dad to Spokane with a pickup truck load of our belongings. They arrived under a cloud of ash shortly after the Mount Saint Helens volcanic eruption on May 18, 1980. They found an apartment and unloaded our boxes and mattresses. My father-in-law tried unsuccessfully to convince Steve to change his plans, convinced that the ash was detrimental.

A more pressing issue was getting court permission to take Michael out of the state, as Fred's family was contesting our move. The judge ruled in our favor, citing advantages to Michael in moving with his new stepdad and me and starting a new life. Unfortunately, it was a $500 expense we weren't expecting.

We were eager to move forward with our plans. *The Spokesman Review* arrived weekly, informing us of events and activities happening in the town we were moving to, and a post office box was secured to forward our mail to. I didn't stay for the graduation ceremony, as I was eager to start my new job.

I stopped to say goodbye to Mom the day before we left Duluth. I tried calling her first, but no one answered. I knew I'd regret not stopping by and took the chance, knowing she would hurt my feelings and turn me away to appease Don. My house had been emptied, and Kay, my maid of honor, was letting us stay with her before leaving town. After I knocked on the front door of Mom's bungalow, I heard the living room window slide open and Mom talking in a loud whisper through the screen. "I can't let you in. Your father doesn't want anyone here. I can't help it, Debra, he's sick. You're a nurse, you should understand. Everything bothers him. I can't even run the vacuum."

Rather than step outside to say goodbye, she shut the window, turned her back, and walked away. I should have expected it. We were like strangers. I didn't understand why, so I blamed him. He was always jealous of any time we spent together. Grandma said she lost her daughter, my mom, when she married Don.

New Beginnings in Spokane

All our belongings were either in our new apartment in Spokane or in our recently purchased $400 station wagon, packed and ready to go. I held a rummage sale, sold my sofa and appliances to friends, and gave Michael's swing set to a neighbor. I promised myself I would strive to be content with no more than what we had. However, I didn't like the idea of living in an apartment. Having my own home for the last seven years had provided the stability I craved after moving over fifty times during my childhood.

Years earlier, when I divorced Fred, I had almost lost my home when I entertained the idea of giving it to Fred in the divorce settlement. The experience of trying to find an apartment during that time dissuaded me from that course of action. A nosy, older woman who didn't like single moms interviewed me. She was renting out a dilapidated apartment for more than the cost of my house payment, taxes, and insurance combined. I remember her prying questions: "So, you're not married? And you have a kid? Why would I rent it to you? You're just welfare trash."

I never wanted to go through that again. That experience motivated me to petition the bank to refinance the house in my name and take out a little equity to repay my ex-in-laws for the original down payment and appliances. The seven years I lived there provided stability and comfort.

After selling my Duluth house, I started spending my days off work house hunting in Spokane. I connected with a real estate agent I had met through the Spokane Chamber of Commerce when I was planning my spring interview. He had driven me to and from the airport and hospital for my job interview. In retrospect, at age twenty-three, I was naïve and very trusting. He found us a house for $35,000. The seller agreed to finance our loan at 10 percent interest, way below the 16 percent conventional mortgage interest at the time, with a balloon payment due in three years after Steve's graduation. We moved into our three-bedroom bungalow near Shadel Center the month before law school started. Steve painted and removed the old carpet, exposing original hardwood floors. We had money left from selling our Duluth house to buy furniture. The desk with a new manual typewriter was placed in the dining room for Steve. We took the smaller bedroom at the back of the house to avoid traffic noise, since I'd be working night shifts after completing the new graduate training. Michael had the larger front bedroom. The third bedroom and laundry were in the basement.

REFLECTIONS

Locating the source of blood loss in stage one of wound healing is an essential step in minimizing blood loss and progressing to the next stage of healing. Without the benefit of our longstanding friendship and Steve's transparency and openness, I might have questioned his sincerity and missed the opportunity to recognize the source of my woundedness: unresolved trust issues and poor self-esteem. My wounded self-esteem drove a wedge between us. I'm grateful for Steve's positive self-esteem and self-respect, which led him to issue me an ultimatum. This was the first of many lessons I'd learn from him. Having time between letters and geographic distance between us allowed for a more thorough and thoughtful reflection of my circumstances and our relationship. His love filled a hole in my heart that I didn't know I had.

CHAPTER FOUR

SECURING AND SEALING

Spokane, Washington, Winter 1980

I was seated alone across from my doctor at an imposing wooden desk. Steve was in class. I braced myself for the hysterosalpingogram test results, eager to know if my fallopian tubes were blocked, eliminating all hope of getting pregnant. I believed the results would decide the fate of my marriage. My doctor's words caught me off guard, like a slap to the face. The cold and detached way he relayed the unwelcome news seemed surreal, making the news even more painful and difficult to grasp.

"Your tubes are completely blocked on both sides. Pregnancy is not an option."

No hugs or comforting words like, "I'm so sorry to have to tell you this." Then he stood up and directed me to the lobby.

I stepped outside into cold, wet, and icy snow flurries in downtown Spokane and walked to my station wagon. The heater didn't work, so I shivered all the way home while trying to hold back sobs. As I reached our driveway, I pushed away my sadness and searched my mind for something positive... and found it. We no longer needed contraception, and I was incredibly grateful that I hadn't given Michael up for adoption. I was also thankful for his grandparents' pressuring us to keep the only baby I would ever have. I wondered if I was being punished by God for having an illegitimate baby, for divorcing, or for having sex outside of marriage. The guilt and shame returned and compounded the grief of infertility.

After finishing the new graduate nurse program, I started working ten-hour night shifts in the ICU. No longer was I the confident LPN working as a float nurse. Instead, I was a novice registered nurse out of her comfort zone, caring for the sickest patients in a major trauma hospital. The constant stress from responding to life-threatening injuries, surgical complications, emergency resuscitation, and continuous monitoring of everything possible to be monitored was wearing me down.

Work tension followed me home and occupied my dreams. On several occasions, I found myself sleepwalking through the house, confused about my whereabouts, in search of a patient. I searched frantically from room to room, wondering why I couldn't find that patient who needed me, whose life depended upon me. I felt desperate, anxious, and almost hysterical. As expected, job stress increased even more after the residency ended and I was no longer assigned a preceptor.

I found myself recalling Sr. Helen Clair's hesitations about advancing me into the RN program when she suggested my LPN role might hold me back from thinking like a registered nurse. Her concerns were realistic. Working with critically ill patients requires split-second decisions and quick responses, with little time to consult with physicians. Compared to an LPN, I was trained as an RN to be an independent critical thinker, to lean less on others. More importantly, I needed a positive mindset to believe in my abilities before I could act on them, and I needed to interact with physicians and family members differently, to be more proactive and confident.

Stress at work, compounded with the heartache I felt in sending Michael back to Duluth for the entire summer, pushed me into deep sadness. The judge's final decision concerning Fred's visitation rights mandated Michael to spend the entire summer and every other holiday in Minnesota. I lost the desire to do anything beyond bare minimum expectations, working in slow motion and feeling numb. Watching television soap operas all day distracted me from my sadness. It also interfered with getting the necessary sleep I needed to be alert at work. I gained twenty pounds and high blood pressure using food as a source of comfort.

My elusive abdominal pain returned on the evenings I was scheduled to work night shifts. To ease the pain, I snuggled with Steve on the sofa in the dark, listening to Pink Floyd. The pain subsided as I drifted off to sleep and returned in time for me to awaken and leave for work. Steve and I slowly adjusted to the expectations of one another as newlyweds, homeowners, and co-parents. However, we did not adjust to my mood changes and depression; we just ignored it.

SLEEPLESS IN SPOKANE

It was 6:00 a.m. and my ICU shift would soon end. I needed to push through and complete the last of my morning duties by 7:00 a.m. and give a report to the day shift. I glanced out the window to find that the dawn's first light was poking through the edge of the night sky. Indeed, the morning sun was struggling in the distance to find its rightful place, pushing out the pink and purple hues.

It had been a busy night, the last of four ten-hour shifts taking care of twenty-seven-year-old Juan. The humming of the morning activities had begun. Laboratory and respiratory technicians were making their rounds from patient to patient, custodial staff were emptying trash cans, with the physicians attending to their hospital patients in time to leave and attend to patients at the clinic. The rise and fall of the ventilator kept time with the steady drip of four intravenous solutions and Juan's heart rhythm, which was amplified by the heart monitor. It was my fifth and final night caring for him before my long stretch of days off.

Bathing was accompanied by joint exercises to prevent his extremities from contracting while he lay peacefully in a coma. Morning meds were administered; antibiotics, steroids, and blood pressure medications were pumped into his veins. Antacids to prevent stomach ulcers were pushed through his feeding tube, and a suppository was administered via his rectum to reduce his fever. Secretions collecting in his tracheostomy tube were thinned with sterile normal saline and suctioned out, clearing his airway for more efficient respirations. The total amounts of fluids administered and excreted over my shift had been measured and recorded hourly to ensure Juan's kidneys were working and I had not overloaded his circulation.

My last three tasks to complete were oral care, dressing changes, and instillation of eye drops to prevent corneal abrasions. The coma caused him to stop blinking, limiting his tear production, requiring the administration of artificial tears every four hours. I carefully placed all the necessary items in a tray at the head of his bed next to the humming ventilator. The dressing changes were completed with the application of Benzoin tincture, an adhesive that held the edges of the bandages in place. Soft pink sponges embedded in powdery toothpaste were dipped in water and brushed across Juan's teeth and gums. Last, I reached for his tube of eye drops and prepared to administer them. I suddenly stopped, panicked at the thought of what was about to happen. I couldn't believe that I had almost glued his eyes shut with the tube of Benzoin instead of his artificial tears! The two containers were the same size, shape, and color. My mind exploded, and my heart pounded at the realization of my near mistake. In an instant, I knew the source of this near-tragic moment. My almost error was most likely the result of not having enough sleep. Either I wasn't as alert as

I should have been, or I was distracted, thinking about what needed to be done when I got home. Indeed, a contributing factor was the similar size, shape, and color of the glue and eye drop bottles. At 7:00 a.m. I reported off to the day shift nurse before leaving to catch a city bus ride home. In retrospect, I should have come forward to perhaps prevent a potential future error by another exhausted nurse looking at similar containers, but I didn't.

When I arrived home, I went straight to the bedroom, stripped out of my scrubs, and climbed into my unmade bed, too tired to shower. Four hours later, I was wide awake and without an ounce of energy. My heavy legs propelled me as I wandered from room to room, trying to generate steam to launch me into a productive morning. It was eerily quiet, and I was lonely. Michael was in Minnesota, and Steve was clerking at the law firm for the summer. He'd be gone for hours. My only friends were nurses at work and those in the Washington State Nurses Association (WSNA), a professional nursing organization and union. I had volunteered to update their membership roster, but I lacked the interest and energy to work on it. Everything I considered doing seemed too overwhelming and burdensome. Aside from people at work, our retired neighbors, Howdy and Francis, and the staff at Shadle Library were the only people I talked to. I missed having friends around.

I needed to get out of the house, to escape what I didn't want to face, so I went for a drive. I didn't know where I was headed as our yellow '72 Datsun Honeybee backed out of the driveway. Tears started flowing as I thought about the previous week. Both the finality of the infertility diagnosis and the news from the insurance company. They hadn't approved surgery to unblock my tubes, which was a huge letdown. I was frustrated. Steve said he'd write a letter on law firm stationery to appeal the decision. We were approaching our second anniversary, and we were both unhappy. I harbored guilt for us not being able to have children together. Money was tighter than expected. Steve's student loan wasn't going to cover everything. We would have to start setting aside money for next year's tuition and the bar review course. The commitments between law school and our jobs left little time to enjoy each other. He was gone so much that I checked up on him one night at the law library, needing assurance he was really studying. Fortunately, my insecurity, fear, and distrust evaporated upon seeing he was in fact at the library, oblivious to the rest of the world, with his nose in a law journal, stopping periodically to scribble notes.

As I continued driving along the interstate, I thought about how my job stress revealed itself in my dreams. One night, Steve woke up to me straddling his body, staring at the TV screen on our dresser, screaming, "There's no rhythm, I'm starting CPR!"

He threw me aside just as I was to begin compressions. Another time, he woke up to me kneeling next to the bed holding his arm, saying, "I need to restart your IV; it will hurt for just a moment."

I'm not sure what was worse: the lack of sleep or my nightmares. In addition to ICU dreams, I was waking up in tears after dreaming about Don. Leaving Duluth didn't seem to have helped me escape the pain of my family drama and dysfunction.

I had to regain my composure before driving back home. I didn't want Steve to see me crying. I was embarrassed and ashamed to admit how sad I had become. Forty minutes and forty miles after leaving home, I was crossing the state line approaching Coeur d'Alene, Idaho. I needed to feel better and get rid of the pain, the tightness in my throat, and the tension in my neck. I convinced myself I couldn't go home yet. I needed help. I drove around until I found a phone booth, parked the car, and with both determination and trepidation, placed a call to a local inpatient psychiatric center a few miles away. I checked in with the receptionist and called Steve to let him know where I was.

The Steve I knew and loved was not the same guy on that call. He was angry and wanted me home . . . now! I was baffled. I expected his education and work as a counselor would have prepared him to receive this call with compassion and understanding. At that moment, I sincerely believed he viewed me as the rock in our relationship, and he wasn't prepared or equipped to see me in any other way. In his mind, I was Debbie: strong, capable, determined, and resilient. Altering this belief was something he seemed unwilling or unable to do during that call. In that moment on the phone, hearing both anger and distress in his voice, I chose to be the caretaker, not the patient, promising I'd be home as soon as possible. I left before the admission was completed.

Six Weeks Later

My unresolved sadness enveloped me like dense fog despite my efforts to rise above it after the failed visit to the psychiatric center. This overwhelming sadness obscured my vision and reality. Six weeks after my drive to Idaho, unable to face the day, I called in sick at work. Michael was still in Minnesota, and his dad wouldn't let me talk to him on the phone. The weight of my loneliness held me down; it was the lowest I had ever been. I felt depleted and empty, hollowed out without any substance left in my chest; it was just a void. Even my breathing felt heavy. My emotional anguish was more than I could bear. I needed the pain to end. Without clarity of mind, I gulped down a bottle of aspirin with a Diet Coke, desperate to make my pain stop.

Steve found me on the kitchen floor and was able to arouse me. I was coherent enough to insist he did not take me to my workplace. He drove instead to the Holy Family Hospital emergency room. It was a humiliating experience. From my experience managing patients who overdose, the care I received was as I'd expect. A tube was inserted into my nose to empty my stomach, and charcoal was administered to absorb the aspirin. The side effects from the aspirin caused a terrible ringing in my ears. I couldn't look the nurse in the eye, as I was too ashamed to face them. The shame came from the belief that 'nurses should know better,' and a parental message that it's shameful to be weak and needy. And last, the Catholic belief that to take one's life is unforgivable.

Upon discharge, I had a follow-up visit to see a counselor the next day. I found comfort and assurance in something the counselor said: The **exact** circumstances leading to my suicide attempt could never be repeated. I knew this was true, especially if I made changes. Our sessions continued for six weeks. They helped me examine my beliefs and what I wanted in life. My depression was temporary, yet I had almost made a permanent, life-changing decision that would have added greater misery to many when I needed only a temporary solution. I was grateful for my access to health insurance and counseling services. I strongly encourage anyone experiencing extreme sadness that lasts beyond two weeks to seek professional services before the feelings escalate and become more difficult to manage, and to **call or text 988,** the national suicide prevention line, anytime 24/7 if you or another is at risk of harming oneself.

We almost divorced during my depression, and I considered moving back to Minnesota. I had contacted Kay to see if the hospital was hiring. During our phone call, she challenged me with a thought-provoking question: "Are you sure you want to divorce a second time and come back here as a single mom?"

Before making any final decisions, I wrote the following in my diary: "I can't believe Steve would give up on us so easily. I thought he was stronger and more committed."

The truth was that he didn't want to fight or argue and just wanted me to be happy. Steve was at heart a peacemaker, and seeing my distress, he gave in and agreed to separation, believing it was what I had wanted. A few days later, we had a heart-to-heart discussion about my sadness and our marriage. Steve admitted he had read my diary and was surprised at my comments, explaining he didn't want to give up on us. "Giving up" was my perception of the situation, not his. Steve's explanation and Kay's challenging question helped me realize our problems would only be made worse if we didn't work through this hurdle together.

SUMMER 1981

During the summer of 1981, I experienced a crisis of faith, questioning my values and beliefs. I questioned my religious beliefs, my faith and purpose, and what really mattered in life. I wondered if my work in the ICU truly mattered. Most of my patients were in a coma or sedated. Unlike my patients in Duluth, I didn't get to know them and seldom saw them discharged from the hospital. Only once in three years did a patient come back to the unit after being discharged; his name was Juan. He walked onto the unit during the evening shift, asking to speak to the nurse in charge. He had miraculously survived a severe infection, septic shock, and near-fatal organ shutdown. Several nurses gathered around him at the nurses' station as he shared his experience as our patient. He recalled people talking and singing, and him feeling cold most of the time. I could hardly believe he was the same young man whose eyes I had nearly glued shut.

I saw more deaths in my first year as an RN than I had seen in five years as an LPN. My way of coping with the stress and pain of seeing so many deaths and serious complications sometimes revealed itself with a jaded or dark sense of humor, like experiences described in *The House of God*[3], a popular book shared among ICU nurses. The finality of death and medicine's attempt to control the timing of death with advanced technology confused and challenged my belief system about God, faith, and the role of medicine and technology in health care. Exposure to patients with religious and cultural backgrounds different from my own also challenged me to understand our differences and similarities in our shared humanity.

I hadn't been to church or opened a Bible since moving to Spokane. I'd grown accustomed to depending on myself and my training and lost interest in the Christian community, deciding most were hypocrites. Television evangelists caught misusing church donations and who failed to follow the doctrines they preached for others to follow had diminished my trust in the church.

My mistrust, arguments about the superiority of each other's theology, and Mom being banned from communion for marrying a Lutheran prompted a personal soul search and study of world religions. I researched several religions, some of which I had never heard of. After studying several "isms": Judaism, Hinduism, Buddhism, Taoism, Jainism, Shintoism, Islam, and Catholicism, I attended a Catechism class to investigate my Catholic roots. Nine months later, after my research and a unique spiritual encounter, I declared myself to be a non-denominational Christian as I saw strengths in many different denominations.

During this time of soul searching, I also read self-help books to overcome my sadness and shame, like I'm Okay You're Okay,[4] Your Erroneous Zones[5], and The Power of Positive Thinking[6]. The shared wisdom of these books contributed to my healing.

Clarity emerged from my confusion about my faith in an encounter with God. I was home alone in the middle of the day, sitting cross-legged on our velour sofa under a large window across from an oak veneer entertainment center. Light danced across the pale gold wall and the TV screen across from me. I was startled by a deep voice calling out from the upper right corner of the wall, illuminated by the dancing sunlight. My eyes immediately searched the wall for the source of the voice.

"You need to get in the back seat!" the voice boomed. I stared at the corner but didn't see anything, and the voice continued. "It's time for **you to let me do the driving."**

I knew at once who it was and what it meant. It was God telling me to let go of trying to control everything and to lean on Him, as I had in the past. The reasons for my recent struggles were mainly due to my own actions. Not trusting my higher power and relying on my own limited means had left me sad, overwhelmed, overworked, and stuck. I felt ashamed of the truth. I had blocked God and my faith out of my life. Like the machines controlling my patients, I was trying to control all of life's variables, and most were out of my control. Following this realization, I prayed for the first time in over two years. I asked for forgiveness for abandoning my creator and the source of my purpose and being. I had created new Gods in my life, distracting me from the love, grace, comfort, and forgiveness of my creator. I had elevated Steve to the position of a God in my life, not recognizing his human vulnerabilities as he struggled with law school, the internship, and being a dad to a child just fourteen years his junior. It was time to reclaim my position as a child of the all-knowing and loving God, and once again embrace the teachings that had comforted and sustained me through my youth.

By fall, we had started attending a church where we especially enjoyed the popular adult Sunday school class, taught by an engaging storyteller of Old Testament stories. The church's women invited me to attend a women's retreat, scheduled on my twenty-fourth birthday. A video of a female Evangelist preaching and sharing stories reminded me that I was special, mattered to God, and was worthy of God's freely given love and blessings. The experience rekindled my desire to reconnect with God through prayer, community, and reading the Bible. Rediscovering these feelings was comforting, and with a greater sense of hope, love, and belonging to something greater than myself. Within weeks, my loneliness melted away, replaced with gratitude and joy. The world seemed brighter, and I felt renewed and hopeful for better tomorrows.

My increased sense of self-worth triggered my desire to care for myself better. For my health, my career, and our marriage, I transferred out of the ICU to the obstetrics and gynecological (OB/GYN) surgery unit. I also relinquished my volunteer duties as membership chair of my local WSNA chapter. Steve and I agreed to give ourselves three months to work on our relationship before making any permanent decisions.

My new job was less stressful, and I enjoyed socializing with my new colleagues on my days off. Several changes occurred with the transfer: the bad ICU dreams and binge eating stopped, and my blood pressure returned to normal. Steve and I started running together for exercise, attending church, and going on dates. I had forgotten how much I enjoyed his company when I wasn't so stressed out.

Three months after transferring, I reminded Steve of our agreement to reassess our marriage. He didn't recall the agreement and was surprised I even brought it up. He assured me all was well with us and insisted we never consider divorce as an option. Steve's easy-going nature returned during his second year of school, and my confidence in both our marriage and my abilities as an RN increased.

A year later, I returned to the ICU. Working ten-hour shifts allowed for longer stretches of time off work, enabling me to take short trips during the summer. I joined an exercise class with friends from work and hosted a wedding shower for my old preceptor. With my new outlook, I realized that Michael's summer in Duluth freed up my personal time to pursue friendships and summer school.

The last two years in Spokane passed quickly. Due to the sluggish economy, none of the law firms had new hire openings, not even where Steve was interning. Two former military personnel and law school buddies suggested that Steve join the military in light of President Reagan's increased military budget. He took their advice and attended officers' training on the East Coast during the summer of '82.

My days were full while he was gone. I worked evenings and

attended a statistics course in the mornings to fulfill a prerequisite requirement for nurse practitioner (NP) programs. On my days off, I hung out with work friends and researched NP programs in Navy towns with warm weather. By the end of summer, I was the charge nurse on nights, mastering medical technology. I learned to operate the balloon pump machine, which temporarily helped patients with weak hearts, and six months later, I took hemodialysis training to help ICU patients with kidney failure. Despite enjoying my job, I became increasingly dissatisfied with caring for preventable patient medical problems with poor outcomes. I was eager to change my focus from an RN to health promotion and disease prevention as a nurse practitioner (NP). This had been a dream submerged in my subconscious since I took the Contemporary Issues in Nursing class, where I first learned about NPs and health maintenance organizations (HMOs) during my senior year at the CSS.

December 1982 Diary Entry

> I don't want to stay working in intensive care, prolonging misery with technology. Some nights I feel as though I'm dialyzing a corpse. I hope to get into an NP program and be able to help people prevent the problems I'm managing in the unit. Got the Jane Fonda Workout album for Christmas from Steve. He remembered how much I enjoyed listening to it at the gym during my exercise class with the nurses.

Life was busy outside of work as well; we had out-of-town guests and volunteer positions. I was Michael's Den leader in Scouts, and Steve coached his baseball and football teams. I had weekly visits to the orthodontist to straighten my teeth in preparation for surgery to realign my upper jaw. The insurance company eventually agreed to cover surgical treatment for my infertility, so I spent time researching surgeons.

I had a consultation with a surgeon who did microsurgery to open the fallopian tubes. Still, I left the visit feeling uneasy about his patronizing behavior and inability to commit to a surgery date. I needed a surgeon available before September, when we were scheduled to move to San Diego. I scheduled surgery in the summer of 1983 with a team of two female surgeons. One of them suggested Steve have a sperm analysis before subjecting me to major surgery. We were shocked to discover Steve had an exceptionally low sperm count, with a five percent chance of getting me pregnant. We decided to focus on my surgery and address his issue after our move. I underwent surgery four days before Steve's six-week Bar review course in Idaho.

Our out-of-town guests were Grandpa Frank, Mom, and Steve's dad, Grandpa Burt. Grandpa Frank sent us money to put a bathroom in the basement as payment in advance for rent. Grandpa Burt remodeled our basement laundry room to include a bathroom, which enabled Grandpa Frank to stay with us in the winter months.

Mom and Vincent took a train to visit us over spring break while Michael was in Minnesota. I was ambivalent about seeing her, knowing I hadn't missed her since the move. Our relationship was complicated for reasons I didn't fully understand. I often felt like I was parenting my siblings and her, and I resented that, along with having to compete with Don for her attention. I couldn't understand why she couldn't stand up for herself and us kids, always giving in to dad's selfish demands at our expense. She often let me down by failing to keep her promises. Over time, I lowered my expectations of her to avoid being disappointed. After Mom returned home, I started having nightmares again about Don, and my sadness started to return. I had to convince Steve I was okay, just sad, not devastated or depressed. After Mom left, I made the following entry in my diary:

I believe mom doesn't feel loved; therefore, she is unable to give or show love. She has no concept of what warm emotions are. I need to avoid deep conversations with her; I should keep them all superficial if I want to avoid disappointments.

Gradually, I came to trust Steve with my family's secrets and disappointments. My decision to be vulnerable and honest with him created a deeper sense of understanding between us, fostering trust in our relationship. It was as though both of us had been rejected in some way, and we clung to each other to give each other strength.

In May 1983, I recorded another insightful thought about Mom and hopes for the future.

MAY 1983 DIARY ENTRIES

Working permanent evening shifts. Enjoyed Kenny Rogers' concert in March.

Steve and I ran in the Blooms Day Run.

A promise to myself: I will not dwell on negative things from my past. No more reminiscing on sad events, it's too depressing, and I can't change them. I must learn to accept the past, learn from it, and keep moving forward with my chin up, keeping an eye on the present and future. No more guilt for not wanting to return to Duluth, and I need to keep my distance from Mom.

I bought a VW camper bus for a San Diego trip in the fall.

SUMMER 1983

Our last summer in Spokane was our best. Steve's graduation was celebrated with law school friends and his parents in our home. He brought me home from the hospital after my gynecological surgery and left for Idaho a day later. It was difficult being alone. I couldn't get in or out of bed, so I slept on the recliner. The surgery was more extensive than expected. The right tube and ovary were removed, and the remaining tube was opened and stitched around the remaining ovary to catch any eggs released monthly. I'll never forget how grateful I was for the kindness of our neighbor, Francis, who brought me home-cooked meals while I was recovering.

We had a plan, combined with faith and optimism, and assumed we'd be in San Diego by the fall. We listed the house for sale, knowing everything was contingent on Steve passing the bar exam. We weren't sure what would happen if he failed. I had saved enough sick and vacation time off to last through my surgical recovery and our departure date. During my time off work, we drove to Indiana to visit Steve's family and picked Michael up in Minnesota on our way home. When we returned home, we accepted an offer on the house and arranged for the Navy to pack and store our belongings until we found a place.

We stopped in Boise on our way to San Diego for Steve to be sworn into the bar. We celebrated, grateful for our good fortune. We stayed in state park campgrounds along the coast all the way to Campland on the Bay in San Diego, where we camped for two weeks while searching for an apartment.

STAGE ONE REFLECTIONS ON AWARENESS

This first healing stage requires a reason for living. I survived childhood trauma, teen pregnancy, a life-threatening pelvic infection, and an attempted suicide by believing I had a purpose that connected me with The Creator, others, and a future. Just as skin cells serve as the first line of protection against harm, sealing and protecting fragile wounds, trust sealed my relationship with the Creator and protected me from harm by securing and strengthening my hopes and dreams for a healthy life. The emotional wounds of shame and guilt triggered my abandoned faith. Confusing the Creator with "religion" and "church" led me not to trust the church or God. Finding clarity between religion and spiritual faith in my higher power renewed my faith and trust in the creator God and my Christian values and beliefs. This, in turn, led to greater self-compassion, acceptance, and forgiveness of my human weaknesses and the release of the shame and guilt that had been separating me from God's love and blessings.

Emotional and spiritual healing in stage one requires **awareness** of or acknowledgment of something greater than ourselves. This higher power provides meaning and purpose in our lives, connecting all of humanity to it, including our unique individual selves.

BURNING

INFLAMMATION

The primary function of inflammation is to increase the supply of blood enriched with healing cells, infiltrating the wound to clear harmful debris damaged tissue and protect the wound from invading organisms. This process is evidenced by wound site redness, swelling, heat, and pain. Just as in wound healing, our greatest and most significant safeguards are in building resistance or protective measures and the elimination and mitigation of harm, which often involves heated situations and pain.

CHAPTER FIVE
SAFEGUARDS AND DEFENDERS

We left for California with a lifetime of biases and stereotypes to shed and new cultures to embrace beyond the experience of my blue-collar, straight, Christian, English-speaking, white background. Before crossing the Golden Gate Bridge, we took a side trip and visited the majestic redwoods in Muir Woods. I felt a sense of calm and serenity as I wandered through the forest, inhaling the aroma of the damp earth. Heading further south towards Santa Barbara, we encountered the remote and rugged coastal cliffs of Big Sur, which stirred both fear and wonder as I clutched the edge of my seat, rounding corners and overlooking crashing waves and extreme depths below.

We stayed with my high school friend Sue and her husband on our first night in San Diego before checking into the campground. It was nice to see a friend from my past after being away from Duluth for almost four years. There was a three-year waitlist for two-bedroom Navy housing units, so we had to manage on our own. We wasted no time in our search for housing, anxious to get settled and start Michael in school. Sue agreed to let us use her phone number on our rental applications. Each rental agent said the same thing: "Leave your application on your way out, and we'll let you know if we're interested in you." No one tried to reach us.

We were excited to be staying in San Diego at the picturesque "Campland on the Bay." Steve and I slept on a double bed, which had been converted from the bench seat in the back of the 1971 Volkswagen bus. Michael slept in the pop-up bunk, and our Basset Hound lay at the foot of our bed. We had a two-burner stove, a small refrigerator, and a water spicket, but no sink. It rained every day in the campground, debunking the myth that "It never rains in Southern California."

It wasn't quite what we were expecting; in fact, it was a muddy mess and too cold to use the swimming pool. After two weeks of living in our camper, we found a two-bedroom condo. Our rent was $700 a month, twice as much as our house payment in Spokane. It was a Navy officer, who was stationed at the same duty station where Steve was to report, who showed us the unit and offered it to us without hesitation. We were in the right place at the right time. That was my first experience of "The Navy Family" taking care of their community. We were relieved to be out of our cramped camper, which was starting to smell like our dog. After a month on the road, we moved in on Columbus Day, enrolled Michael into the sixth grade, and prepared for Steve's departure to Rhode Island, where he would attend a six-week training course for new lawyers. I was determined not to fall into depression by keeping myself busy job hunting and finding a new orthodontist. I was eager to explore our new community with Michael, and the approaching winter *without* snow increased my optimism.

By Thanksgiving, we were settled into our new place. I shopped at the Navy commissary eight miles away. I started working per diem in the ICU at a community hospital near my home. This schedule gave me four days a week off with Michael. One day a week, I saw an orthodontist in preparation for surgery to correct my upper jaw deformity.

Steve was back from the East Coast before Christmas and reported to the Navy Legal Service Office (NLSO). I resumed my daily three-mile runs in our hilly neighborhood, looking south to the mountains in Mexico. On weekends, I ran with Steve around a golf course with year-round colorful plants like birds of paradise, almost fluorescent fuchsia bougainvillea, and an assortment of exotic palms. I felt like I had moved to the Garden of Eden. We jogged effortlessly and in sync around its perimeter.

Six months after my tubal repair surgery, I had a repeat hysterosalpingogram at the Navy medical center. The dye injected into my uterus did not exit the uterus, suggesting my remaining tube was blocked. It was as though I had gone through the surgery for nothing! Despite the disappointment, I was determined that we would have children together somehow. I spent hours on the phone and at the library researching requirements for adoption and foster care. I was frustrated with the application process.

September 1984 was stressful. Michael, now twelve, returned home after the summer in Minnesota, reserved and distant. His father had remarried. Michael's visitation was with his dad and his new wife, not his grandparents. I wasn't sure if his behavior was typical adolescent hormone changes, anxiety over starting junior high, or the new family dynamics in Duluth. Steve, now one year out of law school, was way over his head defending an alleged murderer in a stressful capital murder trial, and I started an NP program. My abdominal pains returned, lasting hours with more intensity. I underwent a gastrointestinal examination at the Navy medical center; the results were normal, but still no explanation.

Dr. PB, my family health nursing professor, lectured on the importance of self-care for our patients as well as ourselves as students, highlighting the importance of sleep, exercise, stress management, and a healthy diet. I took her advice and stopped searching for the best adoption or foster care opportunities. I recall the day I stopped searching; it was in the morning after working all night. I was wearing green scrubs, kneeling by my bed as the sun shone through the window. I told God I was tired of trying to figure out how we could have more children together; that I needed to surrender control to Him. "God, I give this up to you and accept whatever Your will is for us."

It was a relief to let go and focus on school. Another way I managed stress was to continue jogging two to three miles a day.

Early in the nurse practitioner program, my new orthodontist, Dr. J, knowing I planned to start NP school, introduced me to one of her patients, Kate. I remember the day I met her. She appeared to be in her mid-thirties with short curly brown hair and large plastic-framed glasses. After we were introduced, she stood up and stepped away from the exam chair, faced me, extended her hand holding a business card, and said with a smile, exposing her shiny braces, "If you ever need a preceptor, please give me a call; I'd be happy to help you."

I thanked her, not knowing the goldmine I had just been offered. Her card indicated she was a family nurse practitioner with a master's degree in nursing. That card remained in my wallet until it was time for my first clinical course, when I began examining patients in the clinic. The course, advanced health assessment, included classroom lectures and a lab where students practiced examination techniques on each other under the direction of faculty in a classroom followed by real-life patient encounters in the clinic. Kate became my preceptor, overseeing my real-life patient encounters and teaching me interviewing skills and health assessment techniques.

During the following three semesters, Kate continued as my primary care preceptor, teaching me the critical thinking skills necessary for forming a diagnosis and treatment plan. When clinical placements were needed for women's health and pediatrics, she happily referred me to her colleagues, a nurse midwife and a pediatric nurse practitioner. As a newcomer to Southern California, the chances of finding my own clinical preceptors were slim. I look back on my encounter in Dr. J's office with gratitude and believe it was a gift from God.

When I met Dr. J, I was not aware of her highly respected and professional relationship with Navy oral surgeons. It was a huge advantage to me, as they respected her work. Our relationship continued for thirty years until the month she died in her eighties. She was my son's orthodontist, and she put a second set of braces on me in 2007 after I developed a complication from jaw surgery.

My NP training provided advanced training in three core areas: physical assessments, pharmacology, and pathophysiology. During advanced health assessment, I practiced conducting a male exam on Steve and discovered the underlying cause of his low sperm count: scrotal varicoceles. Slowly, my skill set began to cross over into those of the medical profession as I learned how to diagnose medical conditions and prescribe medications, treatments, and therapies. My confidence as an RN was growing as my insecurities as an NP mounted, knowing how much more I needed to learn. It was overwhelming at times, but my mentors guided my progress and kept me focused.

The NP program trained us in many areas beyond direct patient care. We learned to evaluate and apply scientific evidence to improve patient care, and decisions affecting patient care policies, procedures, interprofessional collaboration, and leadership skills were taught and modeled at school and in the clinic. Health promotion and disease prevention modalities across all age groups were integrated across all our classes. I was grateful to be a student at a pioneer organization in the health maintenance organization (HMO) movement, with an emphasis on preventive care to keep patients healthy and control medical costs.

During my first semester, I met another student who was a supervisor at a home health care agency, who offered me an RN job working days whenever I was available. I was tired of working twelve-hour nights on weekends, so I accepted her offer. I covered a large geographic area, encompassing both affluent and disadvantaged neighborhoods, from the coast to several miles inland. Being able to park the VW bus on the beach in December during my lunch break, soaking in the sunshine while listening to the waves between patient visits, was a sweet experience for a girl from Minnesota. That was one of the perks of my new job, along with working days, getting paid to drive, and discovering new neighborhoods. Less of a perk was visiting impoverished families living in overcrowded conditions and relying on interpreters when caring for Spanish-speaking patients.

I noticed unusual breast tenderness in my second semester of the NP program. I assumed it was premenstrual tenderness. I reluctantly bought an over-the-counter pregnancy test when my period didn't come. I didn't want to get my hopes up or Steve's, so I didn't mention it to him. I knew it was improbable that I was pregnant, as my one tube was blocked and his sperm count was extremely low. I used the pregnancy test on a day I wasn't working or in class. I planted myself in the tiny bathroom between our two bedrooms and waited for the results. Steve was in the kitchen making breakfast. I carefully counted the minutes leading up to the results that showed . . . I was pregnant! I couldn't contain myself; I ran into the kitchen, jumping up and down, and screamed, "OH MY GOD! I CAN HARDLY BELIEVE IT! WE'RE GONNA HAVE A BABY!"

Miraculously, I was pregnant!

Once a Navy physician confirmed the pregnancy, we applied to Navy Housing for a three-bedroom unit to accommodate our growing family. We were approved for a home in the officers' quarters, but we couldn't move in until after the baby was born in late November. I was ecstatic and sure everything would go well. Feeling positive and hopeful, I enrolled Michael in middle school near officers' housing in September so he wouldn't have to transfer when we moved. My pediatric rotation just happened to be near the middle school, so I dropped him off and picked him up on my way to and from the clinic.

On Halloween, during my pediatric rotation and a month before my due date, I had the worst headaches I had ever experienced. The pain continued to nag me late into the evening, walking through the neighborhood, watching Michael run door to door trick or treating. Shortly after we returned home, I went into labor. Upon arriving in the emergency room, my blood pressure was elevated, a symptom of pre-eclampsia. I felt so stupid for not connecting the headache symptom with my pregnancy and not checking my blood pressure at the clinic earlier in the day. I knew it was important for the baby to be delivered as soon as possible to avoid developing eclampsia and seizures, dangerous pregnancy complications. Steve stayed by my side the entire time. His most recent work for the Navy involved medical malpractice claims, primarily in obstetrics and pediatrics. He was more concerned than he let on as he closely monitored my progress.

Two weeks after our daughter was born, during Thanksgiving break, we moved to Navy housing. I still remember unpacking dishes with my new baby girl cradled in one arm, wishing we could have moved before she was born. Our new three-bedroom rambler had an attached garage and a large backyard overlooking the ocean. It seemed luxurious after living in our 700-square-foot condominium.

Connie, a fellow student and a new mom, lived nearby. She became a valued friend. The week I returned to class, she warmly welcomed our daughter Michelle into the world with a baby gift. I couldn't help but notice the differences between my two pregnancies and delivery experiences.

The stigma surrounding my unwed motherhood had sparked shame that wounded my soul. That birth experience occurred in a cold, sterile hospital. Nature did not run its course there; the doctor did. He was a general practitioner, trained before the requirement of residences, which now follows medical school graduation. My body was shaved, and my bowel and bladder were medically evacuated. During the middle of a contraction, I was told to lift my bottom and move from a gurney onto a cold steel delivery table. I was strapped in and injected with a narcotic, making me unable to participate in the delivery. Forceps were used to extract my son, tearing my flesh as he surfaced. No one was present to comfort me, as no one was allowed in the labor or delivery room. I was sequestered in a private room to provide privacy as I was placing the baby for adoption. I stayed in that maternity ward for five days following his birth. Those days were sad and grief-filled, with nothing to celebrate. Then, as I exited the hospital, I faced below-freezing temperatures, the onset of a blizzard, and many cold shoulders.

My pregnancy in the 1980s was managed at the Navy base by a nurse practitioner specializing in obstetrics, and my delivery was managed by a physician who, following medical school, completed a residency in obstetrics. My birth experience was joyous despite my pregnancy complications. The treatment included medications and medically induced labor to help lower my blood pressure and prevent the onset of seizures. The delivery was swift, allowing no time for pain control. I was alert. Alert enough to chastise my husband for suggesting incorrect instructions because he chose to read the Lamaze book during labor rather than attend Lamaze classes. He was present in both the labor and delivery rooms and was highly protective of me. My daughter was born at a World War II-era hospital where twenty beds lined the labor room on each side of the ward. I could hear women crying out in pain in multiple languages as the flimsy curtains between hospital beds offered no privacy.

Tears of joy streamed down our faces as our miracle baby was delivered. Our obstetrician commented that she had never seen parents react to childbirth with as much emotion as Steve and me. We were ecstatic, and it was difficult to hold our euphoria. Our daughter's first feeding was by her daddy, as I was too sick to care for her. I began breastfeeding the next day.

We walked out of the medical center with temperatures in the seventies and headed to the beach for a walk along the water's edge before heading home, where Michelle was greeted by her fourteen-year-old brother. We walked in silence for the first five minutes along the shore, collecting our thoughts and reflecting on the recent events that seemed to have taken us by storm, as she was three weeks early. Our prayers had been answered, and our marriage had endured a rocky beginning. Life was good in California, and we were grateful for it. This was no accident; it was our blessing and a reminder to me of the power of faith and trust in the Creator. Our silence was broken as Michelle stirred in her straw basket, letting us know she was hungry.

I completed the NP coursework and the clinic hours necessary for the fall semester within a week of Michelle's birth. The contrast between my two postpartum experiences was as striking as the contrast between pregnancies. Michelle was expected and welcomed by my fellow students and nursing faculty. I was grateful for their support, allowing me to breastfeed between classes. To allow more time with Michelle, I cut back on my school commitments, extending the time to graduate by seven months, which resulted in a partial loss of my financial aid. I applied for and received federally funded low-interest student loans for nurses to compensate for the loss.

In the spring of 1986, Steve was asked to transfer to Lemoore Naval Air Station in Central California. It was a fantastic opportunity for his career advancement. He had one day to decide. However, the move would mean I wouldn't graduate in 1987, and it was unlikely I'd find a school to transfer to so late in the program. The next day, he told the detailer, "I can't possibly uproot my wife right now. She has one year left to complete a nurse practitioner program. However, if you ever have an opening at Miramar Naval Air Station, I would love to be considered for that."

I was both grateful and sad for the decision he made, as I knew it would be a good career move for him. A few months later, the same detailer contacted him, asking, "Did you mean what you said about wanting the base attorney position at Miramar? I have an emergency opening there and need someone right away."

Without any hesitation, he accepted the transfer offer and stayed there for three years. He now tells me that those were the best years of his career.

Mom and Vincent visited over Christmas break of '86. We went to Tijuana, SeaWorld, the San Diego Zoo, Disneyland, and shopping malls. Mom was her usual self, displaying little emotion except for her usual anxiety. I hoped she'd relax once we got to Disneyland. Watching her at Disneyland revealed her rigid personality, lack of humor, black and white thinking, and discomfort trying new things; all behaviors I hadn't noticed growing up. We entered the main gate and walked down Main Street USA a short distance and stopped at a café so Mom could have a cigarette and a cup of coffee before proceeding.

Looking ahead toward the crowds leading to the Sleeping Beauty castle, Mom said,

"You guys go ahead. I'll wait here for you until you get back."

There was no way I was leaving her behind after buying everyone's ticket and spending almost two hours in traffic. I knew the park was an all-day affair, so I had to get Mom on board. She was overwhelmed and clueless about the park's offerings. I showed her the park map and convinced her just to start one section at a time. Once we got through the Bear Country Jamboree, she was smiling and began to enjoy herself. Michael and Vincent ran ahead and checked in with us periodically. It was a long day; we returned home at about 10:00 p.m. I was glad Michelle was with Steve, and I hadn't brought her; it was hard enough managing Mom and the boys.

I was looking forward to downtime with Mom, to visiting without the distractions of being a tour guide. I wasn't sure why I thought alone time with her would be any different than it was when I lived in Duluth. I guess I was hoping things had changed and I'd feel more connected with her.

Mom wanted to get Vincent some new clothes, so I took them to the mall the next day. We got back to the house in the late afternoon when Don called and demanded that Mom leave the next day. He was tired of being alone. She made some calls to check the train schedule, and Steve agreed to take her in the morning. I was furious; once again, Dad hijacked our time together. I was so disappointed she was leaving in the morning, and I hadn't had any uninterrupted time with her alone. Mom didn't understand my frustration. In her mind, she had checked off all the boxes of what to do in California with Vincent, so it was a good time to leave. She barely acknowledged Michelle or Michael. I said, "Mom, I can't even talk to you right now; I need to go for a run. Would you please watch Michelle while I'm gone?"

She agreed, and I headed to the beach about a mile away. Running had become a necessity in my life, a time to clear my head, make sense of what was going on, and have talks with God.

On that slightly overcast day, while jogging on the beach, I tried to make sense of what I had just experienced. Mom seemed to have an impenetrable wall around her, protecting her from interacting on an emotional level, shielding her from emotional interaction. There was nothing I could do to change it, but I needed to understand it. She had been wounded from an early age, raised by a father who suffered from mental illness, and she had lived in an orphanage. As a vulnerable single mother, she married Don, who turned out to be my physically, verbally, and emotionally abusive stepdad. Mom's thick skin was tough enough to deflect her stressors with the most famous and common coping mechanism: denial. Not being able to share life with her on an emotional level saddened me. Tears trickled down my cheeks at the realization that her visit was a reminder of why I moved away, a decision I didn't regret. It sheltered me from the daily reminders of childhood sadness. Now my concern was that I'd have the same relationship with my daughter, and that frightened me.

Imagine my surprise as I walked into my living room and saw Mom holding Michelle for the first time since arriving in San Diego five days earlier. Mom looked up as I entered the front door and said with a smile on her face, "Debra, she's smiling at me. I don't know why it took me this long to hold her."

"I don't know either, Mom," I replied.

The next day, as Mom was preparing to leave, Michael reached around her shoulders to hug her goodbye. Mom's arms immediately went limp, like a wet rag, and she said with a straight face and her usual monotone voice, "What are you doing, trying to get a $20 bill out of your grandma?"

Michael stepped backwards and looked at her in shock, "Why would you say that?"

I'll never forget that interaction; it was pure and honest on Mom's part. She honestly could not read Michael's sincerity and assumed he wanted something from her, most likely cash.

My final year of NP school was hectic and constantly in flux. Michael was on the high school football team during the fall semester, and I was the booster club secretary. Steve coached Michael's Pony League baseball team, so we spent a lot of time at his games. I was once again working part-time at the ICU at a small community hospital near home. The job was significantly less stressful than working at the hospital in Spokane.

My jaw surgery was completed during Christmas break, my senior year. Michelle was fourteen months old. The pregnancy and breast-feeding had delayed it by almost a year. Dr. T.D. and his team at the Navy Medical Center surgically transformed my upper jaw by making it wider, advancing it forward to align with my lower jaw, and shortening it to reveal less upper gum. The skin on my face was lifted and pulled back to access my jaw and make surgical incisions. To avoid the look of sunken cheeks after moving my upper jaw forward, cheek implants made from donor bone were inserted. The precise cuts in the bones were secured with permanent surgical screws. This was followed by wiring my jaw shut for six weeks while the bones were knitting back together. The pain was minimal, requiring only two days of medication to alleviate it. The change in my appearance was astonishing. I was amazed that there was no bruising and only swelling for about a month. I was delighted with the results. No longer would I be camera-shy or disfigured. The class three malocclusion of my jaw had been corrected. The disappointing news was that I'd have to wear braces for two more years. I recovered from surgery and resumed classes to complete my final semester.

My final clinical placement was in a high school program for pregnant minors. I especially enjoyed working with Sandy, the school nurse. She reminded me of my school nurse, Ms. Bujold, but she was younger and prettier. Sandy took a personal interest in her students and their families. She also took a personal interest in me and shared tidbits about her church family. Unlike my own teen pregnancy experience, the students were from diverse cultural backgrounds, and almost all of them intended to keep their babies and enroll them in the school's daycare center. My role was to assist Sandy in teaching well-baby care and to participate in group support classes, which were like Tip's group time at Hillcrest House in Duluth.

Graduation was celebrated with my fellow NP students and faculty on a boat in the harbor. The drive to the marina revealed May's grey skies complemented by the showy lilac colored Jacaranda trees lining the street leading to the harbor. Mom traveled for two days by bus to join in the graduation celebration. I was especially delighted to show her around the beautiful campus overlooking the ocean with the impressive white stucco Spanish-style buildings, red tile roofs, and the

Immaculate Conception Cathedral. The next day, I had a celebratory luncheon at home with friends and neighbors.

I studied for the national NP certification exam in the summer following graduation. In late September, my results arrived. While watching the sunset over the ocean from our back patio, Steve and I celebrated a milestone. My next goal was to work part-time for a health maintenance organization. While waiting for exam results, I continued working part-time in both the ICU through a registry that staffed local hospitals and then part-time as an NP in Women's Health in Student Health at a nearby university.

Finally, in mid-October, I was offered a two-part interview for a part-time per diem position in the Health Appraisal Clinic (HAC), which was part of a large, fully integrated HMO. My interview was to be followed by a videotaped performance evaluation of me conducting a complete patient health history and physical examination of a pre-scheduled patient. The videotaped exam was to be critiqued as part of my employment interview. I had a week to prepare. Fortunately, my mother-in-law, Norma, was in town for Michelle's second birthday. She agreed to be my practice patient. Practicing my history and physical exam skills on her allowed me to get to know her better. She wasn't Steve's biological parent but his cousin, raised with Steve's birth father and grandparents after her mother passed away. She and her husband, Burt, raised Steve from the age of five, when his birth mother was unable to provide for him, primarily due to poverty.

I arrived early for my interview with the department administrator (DA). His assistant, Marcy, a tall, slender woman with dark hair and olive complexion, greeted me and made small talk to calm my nerves. The interview went better than I expected. My student experiences had prepared me for some of the questions he asked, and where to find information in the medical record.

Part two, the videotaped history and physical, began with a brief review of the medical record, noting test results and prior exam notes, before I crossed the hall to meet my patient. I tapped on the door, "Knock, Knock . . . are you ready?" I inquired before entering. "Hi, I'm Nurse Practitioner Palmer. Nice to meet you."

The patient was a healthy-appearing gentleman in his fifties. He was cooperative and pleasant, and assured me he was okay with being videotaped. After reviewing his medical history with him, I completed his exam and reviewed the results with him. He was pleased to learn that his *biological* age was three years younger than his chronological age, based on a formula used to analyze physiological data. The analysis also included recommendations to lower one's biological age, extending life expectancy if appropriate.

My employee physical was completed a week later. Before the physical, I sat through a videotaped welcome message by Dr. Vincent Felitti, Chief of the Department of Preventive Medicine and the Health Appraisal Clinic (HAC). This video introduction by my new boss was the same one presented to all new patients undergoing a physical examination in the department. I was impressed with his professional and compassionate demeanor, which conveyed a sense of authority worthy of respect, as he explained each of the stations I would participate in as part of my exam. The eight stations included vital signs and body measurements, a laboratory blood draw and urine collection, a breathing test, a chest x-ray, an electrocardiogram, vision, and hearing tests. I was instructed to complete my own health history questionnaire, which would be reviewed with me at the time of my physical exam. Dr. Felitti's presence on that video captivated my attention as I wondered what it would be like to work with him. He was handsome, with a debonair quality, tall and erect posture, silver-grey hair, and an olive complexion that contrasted with his starched white lab coat. After my physical, I was surprised to learn that my biological age was younger than my chronological age, and I could be another six months younger if . . . I lost ten pounds. Apparently, Mom was right, I needed to lose weight.

My seventeen months in Health Appraisal were life-changing, both personally and professionally. During orientation, I was required to attend a stress management class that patients were often referred to. In six weeks, I discovered the source of my frequent abdominal pain and unmanaged stress, and then I learned techniques to minimize and prevent the pain. Additionally, I cultivated long-lasting friendships, developed a network of professional colleagues, and increased my confidence as a nurse practitioner. Six months into my new job, I accepted a permanent part-time position that paid $14.19 per hour. The $2.00 per hour reduction in pay was offset by a comprehensive benefits package as a member of the United Nurses Association of California (UNAC), a labor union. The $10 per hour pay cut transitioning from my RN job in the ICU was worth not having to face nightly life-and-death decisions and taking time away from my family on weekends and holidays. More importantly, I was living my dream, working as an NP, in preventative health care.

Eventually, I was recruited to work in Dr. Felitti's musculoskeletal clinic, where I saw patients with chronic pain. It was a welcome change from the routine of doing only physical exams, and it taught me about the connections between physical pain, sleep, our thoughts, and our emotions.

The two most memorable experiences working in HAC happened in my first and last months. During my first month, midway through my morning, I picked up a chart of a single woman in her late thirties who needed a complete physical, which included a pap smear. Most pap smears also included an offer to prescribe contraception or renew prescriptions for birth control pills. After the physical, she replaced her navy skirt and jacket, white blouse, nylons, and flats while I charted her exam results in my office across the hall. She was perched at the end of the exam table as I entered. I sat on a stool looking up at her as I reviewed her normal test results with her. Next, I started a conversation about well-woman care. It went something like this:

"Are you sexually active?"

"Yes," she replied.

"Do you use condoms for protection from sexually transmitted diseases?" I asked.

"No," she said.

"Are you interested in contraception?"

"No, I am not," she replied.

"Oh, you're trying to get pregnant?" I asked innocently.

"Nope," she replied.

I was puzzled, and my confusion was evident on my face. She stared back at me like I was an idiot, or so it seemed. It took me a while, but it finally came to me: "You have a female partner?" I guessed.

She nodded and abruptly stood up and walked out. The realization of my personal biases and ignorance hit me hard. I had a lot to learn.

During the same month, I examined an elderly woman with a peculiar-looking tattoo on her forearm. Innocently, I inquired about its significance.

"That's from my time in the concentration camp," she said, staring off into the distance.

I wasn't prepared for her reply; it stung as I recalled documentaries of emaciated Jewish prisoners freed from the concentration camps. In that moment, I was invited, momentarily, into her sacred personal pain, stirring in me compassion for her and the others I would never meet, reminding me of our shared humanity.

Many years later, as a faculty member teaching a women's health class, I discovered the standard practice in conducting a sexual history changed to include the following questions:

Are you sexually active?

With men, women, or both?

How many partners in the past year?

Answers to these questions and a few related to IV drug use and transfusions reveal risk factors for sexually transmitted diseases as well as acquired immune deficiency syndrome (AIDS) and human immunodeficiency virus (HIV).

My second most vivid memory was when I told Dr. Felitti I was leaving the department. His response was something like, "So, you're going to work with the worried well in primary care?"

He was surprised to hear I had not taken a position in Primary care; rather, I had accepted one in an orthopedic department. He suggested orthopedics might be more fulfilling than primary care because I'd be more likely to make a positive difference in orthopedics. I felt as though I left with his blessing. Years later, after the publication of his famous research, "*The Adverse Childhood Experience (ACE) Study*",[7] I discovered the source of his seemingly skeptical comment and the relationship between primary care interventions and chronic diseases.

JANE

Many of the nurse practitioners who started their careers working in HAC remained friends outside of work for over thirty years, in part because of the efforts of Jane and Marcy, two of my dearest friends. Jane, a single woman in her fifties from New York, was opinionated with a big heart. We spent our lunch hours together, walking for exercise as we cultivated our friendship. It wasn't long before Jane inquired about my faith experience, asking a few personal questions and offering a suggestion. In her blunt New York accent, she asked, "Are ya a Christian? Where do ya fellowship?"

When she discovered I did not have a home church, she admonished me. "You need to be in a fellowship community," she said with conviction.

Her challenge prompted me to investigate churches near our new home in the Navy housing area. Jane was living at a pregnancy care home for unwed mothers, working night shifts as a house mother when we met. We bonded instantly when I shared my experience at the maternity home with her. Through the years, Jane challenged my faith journey, celebrated life's highs, and supported and comforted me through life's lows. She was our daughter's Godmother and spent Christmas Eve with my family for thirty years, until I moved to Northern California.

I consulted with Dr Felitti through the years as I pondered topics related to childhood obesity while advancing my education in 2008 and again while working on my PhD. Dr. Felitti was generous with his time. We met on a university campus in the Faculty Club, where he shared his experiences leading up to and after coauthoring the famous Adverse Childhood Experience (ACE) Study, which discovered a correlation between childhood abuse and neglect and the development of chronic diseases later in life. In 2012, he introduced me to the work of Jane Stevens, publisher and editor of www.accessesconnection.com, which was later converted to www.acestoohigh.com, a platform that includes both positive and adverse experiences. He recommended I contact Dr. Nadine Burke Harris, an enthusiastic pediatric trauma researcher, for possible collaboration opportunities while I was completing my PhD. I never connected with Dr. Harris. However, her TED Talk about ACEs[8] became a course requirement for a course I eventually taught. I believed it was important for my students to understand the relationships between children exposed to toxic stress and the development of chronic diseases.

Orthopedics

My plan to apply to the Primary Care clinic changed when I learned about a part-time position in an orthopedic surgical care center close to home. I was ready to try something new, and I had experience in orthopedics as a registered nurse. I interviewed for the job with Dr. Charles, the first and former chief of the department. We met in the foot clinic, where he worked with a podiatrist. His specialty was foot and ankle surgery. If hired, I would work with the two of them, seeing patients with foot problems. He was in his fifties, balding, and overweight. His wire-rimmed glasses framed his engaging, large blue eyes. Once we were seated, he gave me his full attention, noticing my sensible grey flats and conservative two-piece gray suit. His expression was serious when he opened the interview with the one question I hadn't anticipated: "Why should I hire you instead of a physician assistant?"

I was forced to defend the merits of hiring a nurse practitioner over a physician assistant. I replied with what I believed to be two benefits of an NP over a physician assistant (PA). NPs practice under their own license and code of ethics, rendering themselves, in addition to the supervising physician, accountable for their actions and outcomes. I also commented on NPs being an extension of the patient, not the physician, like PAs, which sparked an argumentative tone from him. At the end of the interview, I was exhausted and convinced I wouldn't get the job. However, the following week, I was offered the position.

Years later, while having dinner with several colleagues celebrating Dr. Charles's birthday, I asked him if he remembered that interview and why he hired me.

"I had to know how you would conduct yourself in a difficult conversation with other surgeons as well as patients. I intentionally created the conflict during our interview. It's a common way to identify qualified candidates."

He also said he relied on personal recommendations over those from strangers, and a physician friend from HAC recommended me.

REFLECTIONS

At the early onset of inflammation, our body defends itself by transport-ing an army of immunity cells through our blood vessels to eliminate harmful debris and invading organisms at the wound site, creating pain in the process. The experience of pain has taught me we are wired to avoid it; like when touching a hot stove, we instinctively withdraw from physical pain. Pain motivates us to act. We also employ coping mechanisms to guard or defend against emotional pain, often without conscious awareness. My most profound healing experiences occurred during times of intense pain and suffering. Consequently, I've learned to accept the reality of pain in healing and to face my fear of pain and discomfort. Instead of concentrating on the pain, I look for the healing that can occur or lessons to be learned. Something like "making lemonade from lemons."

An open mind and heart enhance our defenses against emotional wounds and are as important as open vessels are to wound healing. Opening my mind to painful truths, possibilities, and new experiences, and my heart to embrace my values and beliefs, equipped me to over-come painful emotional and spiritual wounds. Clarifying my values and beliefs about myself, my marriage, my role as a mother, and my preferred career path was a crucial first step in my healing process. I had to discover my true self and what motivated my behavior. Recognizing and eliminating unhealthy relationships and false beliefs was just as crucial to my emotional healing as the removal of dead tissue and harmful organisms is to wound healing. Discarding these obstacles of negative thoughts and beliefs about myself opened the flow of forgiveness and healing self-love.

CHAPTER SIX
DAMAGE CONTROL

Orthopedic Life 1987-1998

S teve left the Navy and took a civilian job the same month I accepted the position as an orthopedic nurse practitioner. We used his veterans' benefits and bought a condominium near my new job.

During the first ten years in orthopedics, the opportunities to gain experience were endless, and the learning curve was steep, both professionally and personally. Navigating through challenges in power dynamics, relationships, and my ever-changing role in the department was as challenging as providing specialized patient care. Initially, I collaborated with foot surgeons, providing consultations and managing patients with foot pain or deformities, who were then treated conservatively or surgically. Additionally, I managed patients with fractures of the extremities not requiring surgery. My confidence and comfort in the role increased as my competence and expertise improved.

My comfort was challenged when the administration partnered with a podiatry school offering podiatry students clinical residencies in the foot clinic, replacing the NPs. I'd no longer be working primarily with Dr. Charles, whom I'd grown to respect and appreciate as a mentor and friend. Instead, I would be assigned to collaborate with other surgeons specializing in sub-specialties such as ankle, hip, knee, shoulder, and spine surgery. The change required me to expand my practice. This was the first of several changes made to meet the needs of the department and the patients we served.

With each new change came challenges and disruptions in routines, comfort, and confidence. NPs were responsible for writing scientifically based policy and procedure guidelines for the NP practice. As RNs were hired into the department, it was the responsibility of the NPs to develop RN skill assessment and evaluation tools along with RN policy and procedure guidelines. The tasks of orienting and training newly hired NPs and PAs added additional responsibilities to the NP/PA workgroup. As the patient population grew, more surgeons were hired. Each new surgeon brought individual personalities, practice preferences, and regional practice differences. They also introduced new approaches for old problems using more current medications, advanced diagnostic tools, and innovative surgical technologies.

Two examples of practice changes involve the treatment of heel pain and the diagnosis of hip pain. Patients with chronic heel pain that was non-responsive to rest, shoe modifications, and steroid injections were routinely placed in a full, non-removable plaster cast for six weeks, non-weight-bearing with crutches. When a new ankle surgeon was hired, the customary treatments for heel pain changed. Instead of the plaster cast, he prescribed a removable boot, which the department soon made available rather than relying on the services of a cast technician. This provided patients with the opportunity to bathe, do ankle exercises to prevent stiffness, and avoid the temptation to stick something down the cast to scratch an itch. Eventually, the removable boot became the standard of care for treating many foot and ankle conditions, including my own foot fracture, which occurred shortly after the new ankle surgeon started.

The second practice change involved the use of innovative technology to diagnose and treat non-arthritic hip pain. This change started when a new hip surgeon was hired, and it had a profound effect on me personally. I was seeing patients in the new injury clinic and asked my backup surgeon to help me evaluate a woman in her thirties with seven years of progressive hip pain.

Her symptoms mirrored mine: progressive pain, worse with flexing my hip, sitting, and swinging my leg away from my body. After examining the patient, we exited the room to discuss her case. I could hardly wait to hear his opinion.

"What do you think is causing her pain?" I asked after we concluded her X-rays were normal.

This articulate fellowship-trained hip surgeon, in a matter-of-fact tone of voice, said, "I need to order an MRI arthrogram of the hip with contrast dye to rule out a tear of the labrum before I answer you."

In my seven years of hip pain, I had sought recommendations from a spine and hip surgeon and physiatrist (pain management doctor) without the benefit of a diagnosis, and I had never heard of an MRI hip arthrogram. I knew they were commonly ordered for patients with shoulder injuries. At that moment, I wondered if I had a labrum tear that could be diagnosed with this new study. For the first time in years, I felt hopeful for a diagnosis and a cure for my pain. Our patient did, in fact, have a labral tear and was referred to a specially trained surgeon for arthroscopic surgery to repair and remove damaged tissue in the hip joint.

Eventually, I was diagnosed and scheduled for arthroscopic surgery of the hip. They recommended the same procedure that my former patient with similar symptoms had undergone. The surgery was successful. Within three months, I slept through the night, sat for more than twenty minutes, and was able to walk three miles without pain. Living without pain improved my mood and outlook and provided a more optimistic outlook for my future. I was grateful for my surgeon's skill and my improved outcomes.

In response to the growing challenges for prompt access to care, quality improvement, and improving morale, several committees were formed at work. By 1995, I was facilitating meetings and setting weekly agendas in response to an organizational decision for each department to develop a mission and vision plan for improving their department outcomes. While on the committee, I collaborated with resolute, industrious X-ray and cast technicians, medical assistants, LVNs, RNs, receptionists, scheduling clerks, and administrators in seeking and developing solutions that improved patient care as well as relationships between the various work groups. This collaboration enhanced trust and respect between the committee members and the administrators.

Improving communication between work groups was one of our first tasks. On the suggestion of an ortho technician, a wall of small cubicles was built to hold individual mail slots for everyone in the department to receive written communications. It was an easy fix and worked well until it was replaced by email ten years later. With each success in improving situations and resolving problems, our department grew stronger in solidarity, working together as a cohesive team. I was proud to be a part of the process and looked forward to our productive meetings. My colleagues were like a second family to me.

The demand for more NP/PAs in the department caught my attention during a morning staff meeting. In 1998, the chief of the department announced his goal of pairing each surgeon with an NP or PA. Surgeons wanted more help taking calls in the emergency room, operating room, and with patient care in the hospital and outpatient clinic.

In the years that followed, PAs were exclusively recruited while they were still in school, completing an orthopedic PA residency. Their residency training prepared them to step into a position without the need for additional orthopedic training on the job, enabling them to work nights on call for the surgeons. Surgeons were eager to have their help. NPs had no residency training. My training was on the job, mentored by the various subspecialty surgeons, and up until 1999, I had never worked on-call in the emergency room. During my first night shift, I was terrified of making a mistake and grateful for the supportive and competent orthopedic and emergency room staff of physicians, PAs, NPs, and the orthopedic technicians. They all cheered me on in my new role, teaching and helping me learn to reduce fractures and dislocations.

Eventually, I was comfortable treating fractures in the emergency room and sending them to the clinic for follow-up. The learning curve was steep the first year, especially in managing hip fractures. The surgeons were eager to teach, and I was eager to learn. The greatest challenge was to know when to ask for help. My motto was when in doubt, ask for help. I was familiar with individual surgeon personalities and practice preferences, and I knew who wanted to be called about everything and who trusted my judgment. My eight years of hospital experience as an RN eased the transition into working in the emergency room and hospital.

On the Home Front

I was pleasantly surprised to be pregnant once again around Michelle's second birthday in 1988. I believed it was highly unlikely I would get pregnant, so we had stopped using contraception. The first of three miscarriages occurred shortly after starting work in HAC. I lived in my PJs for a week, oblivious to the California sunshine and inviting nearby beaches. I kept Michelle home from daycare; she distracted me from my sadness. We waved goodbye to Steve, suited in his neatly pressed white Navy uniform, and watched him load his briefcase into the front seat of the station wagon. Michael, who was sixteen, retrieved a Pop-Tart from the toaster and waved goodbye to us as he left for school. Michelle was chatty and wanted me to read her favorite book,

Goldilocks and the Three Bears. Michelle was a talkative toddler with a sense of humor. She amazed me with her antics, acting out the story, pretending to feed me. In that moment, my heart swelled with pride and gratitude for this miracle child; the daughter I had risked my life to have, enduring a ten-hour surgery to treat infertility. In those moments, my stiff neck and shoulders relaxed, and the day brightened, lifting my morning fog of sadness. Knowing Steve had grieved as much as I had accentuated the pain of losing the baby. He stayed strong for all of us and moved on. Today I would do the same. No more looking back at what was lost or could have been. Instead, I'd focus on our blessings.

Another blessing that surfaced during our loss was the birth of a friendship. During the chaos that ensued on the day I was admitted to the hospital for the miscarriage, it never crossed my mind to call in sick. The next day, I was beating myself up for forgetting and felt humiliated at my failure. I'll never forget the kindness of Marcy, the department administrative clerk, as I explained my absence. She shared a personal story, showing that she fully understood and offered sincere assurance that what happened was completely understandable and forgivable and would not be on my record. She offered a pardon when I didn't know how to forgive myself and move on. We bonded that day, and she remains a loyal friend to this day.

Two years later, I had my last miscarriage experience. That experience both angered and grieved me. During a routine OB visit early in the pregnancy, I was told my pregnancy hormones were not rising as they should, and I was told I had a blighted ovum. I didn't know what that meant, but I did what I was told. I drove to another clinic to see another provider, believing I would get help to support the pregnancy. I checked in and was told to undress and get ready for a dilation and curettage procedure.

"There must be a mistake. I'm not here for that; I'm six weeks pregnant!"

The look in the provider's eyes told me what I needed to know. Without further explanation, the realization hit me—I was no longer pregnant. I was horrified, and numbness overtook me as I agreed to the procedure to prevent complications from the retained products of conception. After returning home, I suffered from grief, believing I shouldn't have had the D and C; what if they were wrong? What if that baby was meant to be? Eventually, I let it go.

Within a year, I was pregnant again. My prior unexplained miscarriages led me to believe I'd have another miscarriage, that is, until I heard the heartbeat of my ten-week-old son. The world seemed to be celebrating with me. Our Disciple Bible study class and work colleagues showered me with baby gifts, and Kate, my first NP preceptor, passed on her wardrobe of maternity clothes. Our son, and second miracle, was born, joining his nineteen-year-old brother and five-year-old sister.

While I was on maternity leave of absence, we decided to accommodate our expanding family by moving from the condo to a five-bedroom house close to Michelle's new school. Within a month of moving into our new home, one of Michelle's former preschool teachers approached us about becoming a nanny for us. She moved in and stayed until Garrett started preschool. Having a nanny was a blessing I hadn't expected. Even though I was a part-time employee, I had to be available five days a week and one evening a week to accommodate the frequent changes in my schedule. Scheduling changes revolved around our surgeons' schedules, which were informed by unpredictable patient needs.

Faith Formation

We had joined a church near our new condo when Michelle was three. It was recommended to me by the school nurse at the Pregnant Minor Program, where I was a nurse practitioner student. Teaching Sunday school to children re-familiarized me with Bible story classics and provided an opportunity to participate in children's Christian education. Participating in Disciple Bible Study classes with Steve unified our values as partners and parents and provided us with influential and supportive friendships.

I followed my heart and committed to fulfilling a childhood dream during a Sunday church service. An announcement recruiting health-care providers to join a medical team in Guatemala caught my attention. I was intrigued by the mission for two reasons. I had always wanted to volunteer in medical missions, and I had recently promised Steve I too would go on a one-week trip, like the guy's fishing trip in Mexico he was planning with a neighbor. To relieve him of any guilt, I promised to take a journey of my choosing. Volunteering on a mission trip was far more interesting to me than a vacation. The closing hymn that morning in the mid-1990s was "Here I am Lord." I sang the familiar tune, "Here I am, Lord, it is I, Lord, I have heard you calling . . . ."

I shed a tear and committed myself to joining the medical mission. I put in the application and shared the news with our Bible Study group. The following week, the church secretary called to say there was an envelope in the office for me. It contained an anonymous donation covering half of the expenses for my first of what ended up being three mission trips with the Guatemala Project.

During a civil war from the 1980s until 1996, the Mayan people in Guatemala suffered. The church deployed a team to investigate potential opportunities to help a village of survivors whose entire adult male population had been murdered. The result was the formation of the Ruth and Naomi project. Young boys were taught tailoring skills to create items for sale in local bazaars and abroad, such as backpacks, purses, and camera bags decorated with traditional woven tapestries featuring bright, colorful patterns. The church provided buildings, sewing machines, teachers, and volunteers from across the US to help Mayan families provide income, housing, and health care.

My first mission team included ten nurses and two advanced practice nurses. We provided basic public health care and administered medications to combat parasites, malnutrition, and pediatric infections. Over 900 people, referred to us by local leaders, visited our makeshift clinics in rural churches that lacked electricity and had dirt floors. One memory of a child with an infection has stayed with me for years. I was asked to see him following church service. Through an interpreter, I learned he was suffering from weeks of ear pain. The shy, lethargic seven-year-old allowed me to peer into his ear canal with my otoscope. His bright red drum was draining stinky milky pus. With the help of an interpreter, I provided the family with instructions for taking liquid penicillin and arranged to see the boy in three days. By the end of the week, he was smiling and pain-free. The family's sincere gratitude was heartwarming.

Angel

On our fifth and final clinic day, I examined an infant with malnutrition, who was emaciated and lethargic. She was wrapped in thin cotton gauze, in need of warmth. I removed my T-shirt, printed with an angel across the chest, from under my button-down shirt and swaddled her with it. The warm, soft cotton shirt with angel wings embraced her. She needed immediate attention to survive. We traveled an hour on dirt roads until we reached the hospital gate. Guards in military uniforms bearing assault rifles cleared us for entrance, and we proceeded with mother and baby to the hospital entrance. I said a quick prayer for the baby I named Angel, kissed her on the forehead, and watched as she and her tiny young mother faded into the distance. Angel was one of many malnourished children who prompted the GP to create a nutrition center to be built by the next team of volunteers whom I would travel with a few years later.

The End of an Era: 1999

It was early on a Sunday morning when Mom called and informed me, "I just got off the phone with the nurses. Your father died early this morning."

I knew he had been hospitalized. I had inquired about his condition the night before. His nurse offered to connect me to his room, but I had nothing to say to him. I merely tolerated him for my mom's sake and had stopped trying to have a meaningful relationship with him. Years of hearing him abuse Mom had drawn a wedge between us. I can still hear her begging, "Please don't hit me," followed by a slap. She tried to hide the bruises with makeup, but I knew the truth.

Patiently, I listened as she unpacked the details of his dying moments. Mom, the most unlikely person to offer nursing care, had been a saint assisting him through every chemotherapy and radiation treatment, leading to an apparent cure, until the cancer returned. He would no longer dominate Mom, stealing her joy. A graveside service would be held in the spring.

I broke a promise to never fly to Minnesota in the winter and spent a week with Mom after Don died. The taxi dropped me off next to the dirty snowbank blocking the driveway to Mom's 1970s bungalow. Ten to twenty bulging black trash bags had been tossed in a heap on the front porch; the last of Don's belongings. Mom was dressed and ready to go before I arrived, armed with her usual list of things to do. She looked good; her hair was nicely styled, and she seemed genuinely glad to see me.

"Debra, I just need to run a few errands before I go back to work Friday night. Would you mind driving?"

She usually depended on Dad to do the driving; they both preferred it that way. I looked at her through her Coke-bottle glasses and immediately agreed. We went to the bank, where she opened an account in her name alone and cancelled their joint accounts. Next, we stocked up on groceries. Lee, my thirty-eight-year-old sister, was nowhere to be found and not answering phone calls, just like when our grandma had died two years earlier. She didn't handle death well and coped with a bottle.

On the day before I left town, I stopped at the hospital gift shop and found the perfect gift for Mom. It was a tapestry wall hanging with the following words:

To Everything there is a Season, and a Time to every Purpose Under the Heavens.

I wasn't sure how she would manage without Dad directing her every move. She seemed to find comfort in his dominance. As she read the words on the tapestry, I said, "It's your time now, Mom."

She paused for a moment and nodded in agreement, "It's perfect, Debra."

Don's passing marked the end of a season and the beginning of new ones. I looked forward to having Mom in my life in the new century without his selfish demands. He was no longer a threat like debris, dead tissue, or invading bacteria that interfere with wound healing.

Another new beginning was celebrated when Michael graduated from college, got married, and moved to Northern California. Garrett, a bounding, confident, and curious second grader with a gentle spirit, was his ring bearer, and Michelle, a strong-willed vegan, was a bridesmaid in Michael's wedding. Her decision to "eat nothing with a face" challenged me to be supportive of her independent nature as she entered high school the next year.

Steve and I embraced new career opportunities. After Miramar, he worked as a child advocate attorney until the heartaches of the business were too heavy to bear, and he transferred into a new position. I started working in the emergency room, networking with orthopedic nurses in the hospital, and challenging myself in new ways.

CHAPTER SEVEN

BATTLE GROUNDS

SOUTHERN CALIFORNIA

JANUARY 1, 2000

A new century and era of uncertainty were ushered in at midnight. Conflicts threatened my well-being at home, work, and beyond. By outward appearances, I was doing well. My work evaluations were exceptional, yet something was unsettling. I was never satisfied; I was always striving to do better. At home, the challenges of being a parent were never greater as we strived to advocate for our son at school. For some reason, the insecurities of being a teen mom, feeling judged, and always needing to prove myself surfaced at home and work.

SECOND GUATEMALA MISSION

Carol, a cherished friend and the director of the Guatemala Project, called me with a request that took me off guard. "Debbie, the project has been asked to send another team to Guatemala in the summer of 2000. I'd like you to lead the medical team. We can plan the mission around your schedule."

I paused, knowing the incredible amount of work it would take to recruit and prepare a team, as well as secure the necessary medications to take across the border. Aside from that, I'd need to pay for my travel, room and board, and take time off work. On a gut level, there was no way I wanted to return to Guatemala; it had been an exhausting experience. I had returned home with a bladder and sinus infection, and the place was so darn depressing! It reminded me of my cold and damp childhood, without warm clothes, nutritious food, or healthcare. The experience of seeing extreme poverty and indigenous people being discriminated against triggered my deeply hidden feelings of being mistreated and unseen. I ended the call saying, "Carol, I can't answer you without spending time with the Lord in prayer. Give me a week. I'll get back to you."

Seated at my dining room table, facing the sunrise, I meditated on Bible verses and spoke to God, asking for guidance in responding to Carol's request. The nudge in my heart startled me: "Yes, you need to go; I want you to go."

My first response was indignant, *REALLY? Lord, You know how I feel!* The words on the tapestry I had left with Mom flashed in my mind: "To Everything there is a Season, and a Time to every Purpose Under the Heavens."

Okay, God, I hear you. It's time for another mission trip. When I announced my plans to the family, fourteen-year-old Michelle asked to go with me. She didn't want to be left behind again.

Our experience in Guatemala was a pivotal time for both Michelle and me. The discovery of lead poisoning as a significant preventable public health problem for many Mayans led me to apply to a PhD program in public health. My experience of altitude sickness at 11,000 feet above sea level contributed to my decision to undergo laser surgery on my uterus to eliminate my significant monthly blood loss, which resulted in low hemoglobin levels, causing anemia. The lower oxygen levels at high altitudes and the lower oxygen-carrying capacity associated with anemia contributed to my altitude sickness. I suspect Michelle's experience living in the village may have contributed to her eventual decision to study anthropology.

MISSION AND VISIONS

Facilitating team meetings at work to implement the department's new mission and vision statement inspired me to apply lessons from Steven Covey's books about the habits of effective people and families[9, 10] at home. Our weekly family meetings helped maintain open communication and clear expectations among us. At Michael's insistence, the last line of our family mission statement reads "and have fun doing it," reminding me of the importance of scheduling time for fun and vacations. To keep our lives manageable, we established a limit of two extracurricular activities per child during the school year. Garrett excelled in piano lessons; Michelle moved on to guitar. No longer interested in group activities, Garrett stopped Boy Scouts and basketball. Michelle transferred interest from softball to a swimming club, and we were all doing something at church. All was going well until Garrett's third-grade parent-teacher conference.

Miss Quinn, a thin blond woman in her late twenties, looked me in the face and, slowly shaking her head side to side, said, "He's not doing well, at all. His scores are below average, and he's not paying attention in class. He may need medication," she said in a matter-of-fact tone.

I paused, wondering what she was talking about. Without challenging her authority to recommend medication, I started to doubt myself as a nurse and parent, wondering how I could be so clueless. My memory of Garrett's last standardized test scores being above average brought me back to the present. What could have changed in a year? Alarmed by her comments, we met a week later with school representatives, the reading specialist, librarian, counselor, principal, and his teacher. As we all reviewed test scores, I nudged Steve and whispered, "The only low numbers are the raw scores, not the percentages. I'm not sure what his teacher is talking about."

The principal sensed my concern that Miss Quinn may have been mistaken and asked if I had a question. By the end of the meeting, the consensus was that Garrett was not being challenged in the classroom and that his inattention was likely due to being bored. On the counselor's recommendation, he was administered a test for gifted and talented children. His high scores showed he was a candidate for the GATE, Gifted and Talented Education program. However, there were no openings. Even though the test scores were misread, I was grateful that Garrett's teacher sensed something was off and shared her concerns, and we felt our perspective was taken seriously. This experience led to a successful search for a new home in a school district with a GATE program.

Our local community experienced the shock of another high school shooting five months later. Two students were killed and fifteen were injured. My daughter's best friend attended the school and witnessed the horrific events of the day. Three weeks later, another school shooting occurred at a nearby school; five individuals were injured. A quick responding resource officer de-escalated the situation, and the shooter was apprehended. These incidents did not happen to me personally; however, I was affected by them, my church held a vigil for the victims, and Steve's law office represented the second shooter. I no longer felt safe in my small town.

On the evening of the first shooting, we all slowed down, realizing no one was immune or exempt from such a tragedy. The incident prompted a heartfelt family discussion about the value of life, life challenges, and our need for one another to be present and supportive. It was the perfect time to discuss the logistics and concerns surrounding our upcoming move to our new home. The adjustment would be challenging for all of us. Garrett had been accepted into the GATE program, and Michelle would complete the current year and transfer to her new high school in the fall.

Steve took vacation time at the end of March to move us to our new home, which is ten miles away. Had he been working, he would have been representing the second shooter who eventually committed suicide while in custody. Having represented adolescents and adult victims and perpetrators, Steve taught me that the cycle of violence starts with being a bullied victim. He was glad to have escaped that assignment.

The pain and aggravation of moving was worth the effort. The new place's larger space would accommodate large gatherings and out-of-town guests. The one-acre lot included fruit trees, a pool, and room for a chicken coop. Rather than waking up to the sound of traffic, the "cock a doodle doo" of the neighbor's rooster announced the day. Having been partially raised on a farm, Steve was delighted with his new alarm clock. My unexpected joy was yard work, nurturing a dozen different fruit trees, and the intoxicating scent of orange blossoms. Garrett nurtured a dozen baby chicks and helped create their new home, a five-by-ten-foot chain-link fenced coop with nesting boxes and a tin roof. Within the year, we were blessed with fresh eggs daily, enough to share with friends.

Garrett's middle school science teacher encouraged him to enter the California State Science Fair, and Garrett decided his experiment would involve altering the diet of his chickens to produce larger eggs. We couldn't have been prouder parents as we watched him up on stage accepting the Junior Division third-place medal in the zoology category. He was beaming, and we were proud of him.

Our new home and yard had been vacant and needed serious attention. Working twenty-eight hours a week allowed flexibility in my schedule for house and volunteer projects. Our home improvement projects served as a creative outlet for managing job stress while creating a different kind of stress between Steve and me. My gifts were in decorating, yard work, envisioning the big picture, and drawing up project plans and supply lists. His talents were in carpentry, cement finishing, masonry, and tile work; all self-learned, pacing himself to one project at a time. After a few too many intense arguments and finger-pointing while working on house projects, we both learned to value each other's suggestions and contributions without criticism and to offer grace in the face of mistakes.

While seeing patients in the orthopedic ward, I was introduced to nurses with "ONC" on their name badge, signifying they had passed a national certification exam for orthopedic nurses. To ensure my inpatient orthopedic knowledge was current, I studied the National Association of Orthopedic Nurses (NAON) Core Curriculum for Orthopedic Nursing in preparation for the exam, and I passed. Included with the test results was a request to complete an evaluation of my test experience. In the comment section, I suggested that the Orthopedic Nurse Certification Board (ONCB) consider providing a national exam for nurse practitioners, not just RNs. One year later, I was invited to take part in a three-year collaborative process for developing and implementing the first national certification examination for orthopedic NPs. After the experience, all collaborating participants were granted the title ONP-C, as recognized by the ONCB.

After numerous years of serving on several committees, I recognized the orthopedic department's new vision was becoming a reality. The NP/PA peer review process and RN skills assessment tool for new hires was implemented, providing objective employee evaluations. The Consult Access Committee helped decrease the time gap between the date a patient was referred to and seen for an orthopedic consultation. For example, the backlog of consultation appointments for foot surgery went from six months to three weeks.

The organizational changes improved patient outcomes. Hip fracture rates decreased following the implementation of guidelines for diagnosing and treating osteoporosis. Multiple departments, including orthopedics, participated in developing the guidelines. The NP/PAs assisted the surgeons in developing and piloting the use of a form to capture information about our patients receiving total hip and knee replacement procedures. The data was entered into an electronic database to monitor trends in patient outcomes. This database was instrumental in identifying patients with poor outcomes and the eventual recall of a defective product that needed to be replaced. I loved my work; it was rewarding to know we were making a positive difference in the lives of our patients.

Following my third year of guest lecturing in a nurse practitioner program for Kate, my first NP preceptor and now a faculty member, I started precepting students in the ortho clinic. I enjoyed providing them with a glimpse of my role and the basics of orthopedic care. Working with students in the classroom and the clinic made me a better NP.

One student's experience exemplifies the value of the precepting experience. Doris, the student NP, and I were seeing a sixty-year-old Caucasian female with complaints of knee pain, which was the result of a fall. Our mildly overweight patient was seated in a wheelchair and was too uncomfortable to climb onto the exam table. Her knee x-rays and physical exam of her ankle and knee were negative for fractures or soft tissue injury. Against the patient's wishes, we helped her onto the exam table to evaluate her hip. Flexing and rotating her hip caused pain, suggesting a potential hip issue. We returned her to radiology for hip x-rays, which were positive for a fracture. What a teaching moment, both for myself and the patient. No matter how inconvenient, there is no room for taking shortcuts; always include the joint above and below the affected area, and don't rely on the patient to tell you what's wrong; do your own full investigation. Next, we completed a full admission history and physical and admitted our patient for surgery. Three days later, the patient was discharged from the hospital, and her follow-up care in the clinic was scheduled with the student and me. This was a valuable teaching opportunity to discuss patient risk factors for osteoporosis and hip fractures. Our patient was referred to the osteoporosis clinic for intervention to decrease the risk of another fracture.

2003-2004

Two of our PAs were called to active duty during the Iraq War. Their absence was noticed, as we all added hours to our schedules. In addition to working more hours, the expectations of the NP/PA's role had changed considerably. I recall one of the surgeons telling me, "Debbie, we depend on you to be like one of us in our absence. You're our eyes and ears."

I knew what he meant; however, I was a bit skeptical of his expectations as I had never been trained to do his job or had the experience of orthopedic residency training. Expectations of the NP/PA work group increased substantially along with the hiring of more orthopedically trained PAs, consistent with the expansion of our role in the hospital and emergency room. The added stress was palpable. Rising tensions in the department led to the formation of a much-needed committee to address declining morale. I served as the NP/PA representative on the committee. The meetings revealed the complexities of collaborative relationships between work groups, physicians, and management, as well as the demands on administration from state and federal agencies overseeing HMOs and hospitals.

REUNION FUN

On a hot August evening, while overlooking a nearby golf course, we celebrated our twenty-fifth wedding anniversary. It was a fabulous reunion of family, friends, and neighbors. My dear friend, mentor, and former chief, Dr. Charles, came out of retirement to celebrate with us, along with other friends and spouses from the department. Family from Minnesota made the trip as well, including my birth father's siblings and my mom's brother, Ed, and his family. Garrett's piano teacher, neighborhood and church friends, and couples from Steve's work joined the celebration. We danced nonstop all night with anyone brave enough to join us. Michelle's boyfriend danced with Jane, my friend from HAC, Michael danced with his wife and her family, and our new neighbors danced with each other. It was one of the best nights of my life. Our new home accommodated our out-of-town guests, providing more time to visit with them. The arrival of our sponsors from a Lutheran Marriage Encounter Weekend sparked joy in my heart. We met them on the scuba diving trip in 1984 when I was an NP student. During the NP training, they agreed to volunteer as my case study family for my primary care of the older adult course.

PROFESSIONAL ORTHOPEDIC NURSING

I attended my first National Association of Orthopedic Nurses (NAON) in Phoenix, where I discovered the chapter in my community had dissolved when the former chapter president retired. I contacted her to learn what was necessary to reactivate the chapter. She connected me with everyone she knew from local hospitals who might be interested in reactivating the chapter. I was invested in the process as I wanted nurses at my hospital to be able to network with orthopedic nurses outside our organization in the surrounding community.

I pitched the idea to two NAON members at my hospital, the nursing supervisor and the charge nurse of the orthopedic ward. They agreed to serve as liaison's between the orthopedic nurses and me during the reactivation process. In early 2007, our new chapter was set up as a nonprofit organization with an elected board of directors. To encourage chapter growth, a free ten-week orthopedic nurse certification review course was offered at the hospital and approved for continuing education units for nurse licensure renewal. I developed and taught the course based on the NAON core curriculum textbook.

I was still collaborating with the ONCB to develop the first national orthopedic NP certification examination while seeking reactivation of the NAON chapter. Dottie from the ONCB coordinated a volunteer team of nurses from across the country to develop evidence-based test questions. Our workgroup met in various cities across the country the week before the annual NAON and American Academy of Orthopedic Surgeons meetings. Having ample vacation time, I added an extra day to each of these meetings and played tourist in Washington, DC, Philadelphia, Charlotte, Saint Louis, and Chicago.

I was humbled, proud, and grateful to be a part of the team's historic efforts, diligently crafting test questions. During these work sessions, I discovered most NPs worked in either a clinic, hospital, or surgery center. None of the NPs were working across all three settings. As an employee of a fully integrated health center, I found it more seamless to work across various settings. Three years later, the first exam was offered and approved as an accredited certification examination, a process that must pass scientific rigor. Twenty years later, the exam continues to be updated and provided annually, challenging NPs to keep exacting standards for best patient care.

PREPARING FOR GUATEMALA TRIP NUMBER THREE: 2005

My most difficult mission was the third and final one. The challenges were physical, emotional, and a matter of logistics in securing supplies. Recruiting the medical team was the easiest part of the mission. Our team included two pediatricians, two primary care doctors, a surgeon, three NPs, a returning PA, and several RNs. Half the team was recruited from the HMO where I worked, including Doris, the NP student. They became recipients of "The Everyday Hero Award," provided by my employer, recognizing community volunteers, the following year. Knowing I had a robust team, I appointed myself to be available as backup support to the team and pharmacy clerk. Garrett, at the age of fourteen, joined the construction team of the mission, just like his sister had five years earlier.

The most challenging aspect of the mission was obtaining the necessary medication. My previous suppliers were no longer able to help me. Of course, without medications, we would have little to offer as a team. Feeling hopeless, my anxiety increased with each unsuccessful phone call. Not knowing where to turn, I shut down emotionally and stopped looking for about a week. I didn't have the heart to tell Carol, the director.

With the project weighing heavily on my heart during my morning meditation, I prayed for direction. A voice in the back of my head said, "What took you so long? Did you think you were managing this single-handedly?" I closed the prayer with "May Your will be done," and took on an attitude of expectation and hope.

A few days later, I had a possible lead on a pharmacist with a familiar last name, Johana; I know that name, Lord, where do I know that name from? Then it hit me: years ago, I had kids in Sunday school with that last name. Could he be related to them? I searched my desk and retrieved an old church directory and dialed the Johana family. Mr. Mark Johana, a pharmacist, picked up on the second ring.

" Hi, I'm Debbie Palmer. I was Conner and Mindy's Sunday school teacher in the 1990s. The reason I'm calling is . . ."

By the end of the day, I was jumping for joy, having jumped through the last and most difficult hoop in preparing for the mission. Mr. Johana was able to deliver on his promise. Two weeks before departure, the medications were packed and ready to go. Each team member would check in one bag of drugs en route to Guatemala and return home with bags filled with goods from the Ruth and Naomi Center (RNC). During the holiday season, products from the RNC would be sold at churches by volunteers to secure funds for the following year's mission.

GUATEMALA, AUGUST 2005

With the mission almost complete, grief about Lee hovered over me as I loaded medication bags into the back of the van at the end of the day before heading back to Chichicastenango. Yet, during the two-hour drive, seated in the last row of the ten-passenger van, I got to know Cindy, the pediatrician, and two nurses, Lonna and Laurie. We shared life stories and how we ended up on the team. Cindy had volunteered at Lake Atitlan in her youth, and she was looking forward to returning there with the team on the weekend. It would be the perfect place for R&R at the end of the week. The nurses had heard about the trip through their churches. We talked about our children. I told them about Garrett volunteering on the construction team, painting the school, and installing computer software. I explained his difficult transition to high school, including recommendations for an individualized education plan (IEP) and the challenges he faced in getting the school to honor the plan and in finding proper services for him. Lonna had recently transferred her daughter to a charter school and suggested I consider transferring Garrett there. Laurie worked in the nurse's office at Garrett's current school and offered to drive him to the bottom of our road on her way home. I was so grateful to have these new caring ladies in my life.

One thing I shared with these nurses was a bit more somber: the recent death, just before the mission, of my forty-four-year-old sister Lee. Lee had called me a month before the mission to tell me she was in the hospital with a kidney infection. A week later, she was transferred to a larger hospital, and Mom called me for help in completing Lee's admission paperwork. "Debra, what does do not resuscitate mean? The doctors want me to sign a form that says do not resuscitate."

The question echoed in my head; it didn't make sense. The doctors must have thought she was terminal, that she was not just suffering from an infection. "Mom, there is something more to this. I need to talk to her doctor."

Lee was in a coma with end-stage liver disease and hadn't been truthful with me the month before. Her death, ten days before the trip, was expected, as she'd been transferred to hospice care.

Two weeks before the mission trip, I took emergency family leave from work and stayed in Duluth for four days. My time was spent alternating between Lee's bedside and visiting with Mom and her new husband: my widowed father-in-law, Grandpa Burt. Yup, I'm married to my step-brother. Mom was her usual emotionally disconnected self, seemingly unconnected to the mood in the room.

"I don't have much of an appetite," I said, pushing spaghetti across my plate.

Mom was quick to reply with, "What do you mean you're not hungry? There's nothing wrong with that meat; I used quality ground beef."

Grandpa jumped in and said, "Marie, let it go, of course she's not hungry, her sister's dying."

In that moment of clarity, he helped me connect my emotions to my body and the reality of my grief. An image of my sister from earlier in the day crossed my mind. I no longer recognized her. Her thin and frail body was drowning in the hospital gown, and her head full of beautiful brown hair had been reduced to thin strands. She lay lifeless like a corpse with sunken eyes, yellow skin, and a bloated abdomen. My efforts to connect, as I applied lotion and massaged her back, were futile. I had been on automatic pilot since arriving, almost mechanical, like my mom, holding my feelings within.

My mission teammates offered comfort, assuring me it was okay to be sad and asked how I was managing under the circumstances. They had unexpectedly become the support I had planned to be for them as their mission leader. It was about 10:00 p.m. when I returned to my hotel room. As I drifted off to sleep, I mourned not only the loss of my sister but also the idea I had held onto that someday, after she stopped drinking, we would be close. That possibility died with her.

After returning home from Guatemala, I wanted to learn more about improving public health and had promised myself I'd return to school by the age of fifty. I applied to two PhD programs in public health. The strong letters of recommendation from my two surgeon colleagues and the Graduate Record Examination preparation course were not enough to secure me a spot in either program. I felt rejected, underqualified, and embarrassed, especially by my mediocre GRE scores.

I was also feeling rejected by my NP work group. After two years of petitioning management, with the help of our labor union, the orthopedic NP/PA group was granted what they thought they wanted: a level two status. However, along with the pay raise came the surprising requirement to work weekends, nights, and holidays. I had been instrumental in petitioning for recognition as highly specialized NPs, so I was blamed for the forced change in our schedules. Another PA and I volunteered to pilot the night call shift from 7:00 p.m. to 7:00 a.m. This is when my feelings of estrangement from my NP colleagues began. Other tensions in the department were also noted, as the new manager reduced the budget and staff positions. In their defense, following the Great Recession, the organization had lost patient members, prompting changes from the top down.

Surgeons were also challenged, as the department was adopting a new trauma service. The night shift NP/PA group and surgeon on call would be instrumental in preparing patients for surgery the following day with a designated member of the new trauma team, replacing the old system in which the doctor on call during the night, not the trauma surgeon, performed surgeries on patients admitted during their scheduled call dates. The changes would help patients, surgeons, surgery scheduling, and the department. Complicated trauma surgeries would be performed by a dedicated team with exceptional skills in trauma, not the surgeon on call, who was often sleep-deprived and overworked. Changes were being implemented to enhance the standards of care and efficiency within the department.

A notable change in leadership's tone and their relationship with the NP/PA group was evident during my last few staff meetings. It was adversarial, like nothing I had ever seen before. The chief insulted and belittled one of my favorite PAs, calling him fat and lazy, and the chief intended to track and compare "productivity." The total number of patients seen by each NP and PA after each walk-in clinic would be posted for all to see. My team members were now competing with each other. I was appalled. I knew from experience that not all patient visits were equal in complexity, and patient encounters were never predictable. They could be either quick and uncomplicated or more complex, requiring additional time to be seen. This new method may deter some group members from seeing more complicated patients. Cherry-picking (whether real or perceived) of patient charts was likely to cause conflict. I was not a fan of these changes, and in retrospect, may have been a bit too vocal about it, thereby lessening my reputation as a positive team player.

My opportunity to escape the rising tensions and lack of camaraderie in the department came in an email invitation to participate in a community clinic fellowship, developed in partnership with management and the union. Seven selected NPs and PAs would retain their union seniority, pay, and benefits, which would be funded by the HMO, while accepting a temporary assignment as employees of a local community clinic.

My department chief approved my temporary assignment with

the fellowship. In advocating for the temporary duty assignment, I explained that my salary during the fellowship would not be included in his already approved budget, which meant he could allocate those funds as he saw fit. I said that, not knowing that I may have just shot myself in the foot.

I recall the day I received final approval. I approached him outside his office. He was in a surprisingly good mood.

" Well, Deb, I don't see any problem. I'll sign off on it."

I had his buy-in, and while I hoped to return, I had no guarantee that I would, and I didn't care; I loved the department, but I needed the change and was willing to take that slight chance. Following interviews with the community clinic administrator and medical director, I was accepted and scheduled to start in the spring of 2007, after my planned vacation to Saint Louis, which was the location of the next NAON and ONCB meeting.

Sadness and excited anticipation rolled over me on my last day in orthopedics. A potluck lunch was arranged in my honor, and my colleagues presented me with a beautiful triple-strand pearl necklace and matching earrings as a going-away gift. My final contribution to the department was nominating the orthopedic trauma team for the "Team Excellence Award" in recognition of their innovation and dedication to enhancing patient care and improving work-life balance for the surgical team. Just before I left, I submitted my re-credentialing packet, which the department chief signed, and two supportive colleagues attested to my qualifications for recertification. Recredential approval would allow me to continue seeing patients in the organization until 2010, which would be after my fellowship return date.

I thought of Dr. Charles, my boss and friend, who had passed away five months earlier, and Lucey, my recently retired DA, as I glanced across the parking lot at the recently demolished secondary hospital. They had been instrumental in building my confidence as a nurse practitioner over the previous twenty years. I felt a hole in my soul as I grieved their loss, the passing of an era, and the uncertainty ahead. I had to muster confidence to move forward, outside of my comfort level.

In that moment, I remembered a conversation I had had with Mom after Don had passed. She had said, "It's okay, Debra, change can be good. Everything changes, and we have to go along with it; we don't have a choice."

She was right. I loved my job, but the truth was that my insecurities were the real reason I stayed for so long. I was looking forward to a change.

CHAPTER EIGHT
FANNING FLAMES

MAY 2007

As I stepped off the elevator on the last day of the NAON conference, I got an unexpected call from my son, Michael, in San Francisco.

"Hi, Mom, I need to let you know Michelle was hit by a car crossing the street in front of my apartment two nights ago. She's been in the emergency room with a head injury, and something's wrong with her leg. I've already called Dad; he said to fill you in."

As Michael described the leg injury, I imagined the image of the crushed leg in the lecture I had just viewed, and imagined Michelle in distress. I needed to see her as soon as possible. I left for home on the next flight. My fiercely independent daughter had been on her own since she turned eighteen and moved into a house with four roommates to begin her second year of community college. After graduation, she transferred to a four-year program in San Francisco.

A few days later, I moved Michelle out of her loft and into a house with her best friend. The semester had just ended, and she had pre-planned the move. Fortunately, there wasn't much to move from her

250-square-foot apartment; everything fit in the rental car. I was glad to help, especially since she was now on crutches. We had a pleasant visit despite her injury. I was delighted to meet her best friend and new roommate, who had generously shared her room with Michelle following her hospitalization. Shelly was an answer to my prayers during Michelle's first semester of college in Northern California. During a call home shortly after moving away, Michelle had expressed frustration about being lonely. I ended the call with this comment: "Michelle, I am going to pray for you to meet a nice girlfriend; everyone needs a good friend."

One week later, Michelle enthusiastically described her new friend. Their names were the same but spelled differently; their birthdays were two days apart, and they were the same height and shoe size. They were both blond and blue-eyed, and they were anthropology majors with younger brothers in high school. I was comforted in meeting her new friend but concerned she'd require knee surgery, and anxious to begin the fellowship.

The fellowship arranged for me to attend training to prepare me for implementing a diabetes program at the clinic. I was sent to Park Nichols in Minneapolis and Scripps Whittier Clinic in La Jolla. I absorbed the lecture material and took extensive notes. While in Minnesota, I visited with my Uncle Ed and his wife in a nearby suburb. I appreciated their visit and the break from the classroom.

The changes and complexities in diabetes management, as well as the challenges in caring for patients at low-income community clinics, were significant and at times overwhelming. Caring for patients with more resources and access to integrated care in orthopedics had sheltered me from the needs of patients in the community clinics who had more advanced chronic health conditions and less access to services. Potential obstacles to optimal diabetes management in the clinic extended beyond economic instability, language barriers, and low educational and literacy levels. Added obstacles to care included unstable housing, a lack of social support, transportation, nutritious food, and safe neighborhoods, all of which compounded social isolation and mental health challenges.

The clinic's decision to implement Project Dulce, a culturally sensitive, award-winning diabetes management program, helped mitigate some of the previously mentioned obstacles to diabetes care. The project used Spanish-speaking lay community educators to provide the bulk of patient education. This helped build trust between patients and their clinical healthcare team, comprising RNs, NPs, and MDs. The depth of knowledge and compassion of the diabetes care team amazed me, and I had serious doubts that I'd ever become as competent as they were. Thankfully, I didn't have to be. My role was to set up the program, recruit and admit patients, and orient an RN from Scripps to manage diabetes patients in collaboration with clinic NPs and physicians.

CHILDHOOD OBESITY CLASSES

Shadowing the dietitian in charge of KIDS, a family-focused childhood obesity program, for six weeks was pure enjoyment compared to the diabetes training I had just completed. I was being trained to implement the program at the clinic. It was interactive and entertaining for the kids and informative for the parents. Nadine, a registered dietitian and my mentor, used videos and PowerPoint presentations to teach basic information to parents and their overweight children in a classroom setting. Additional material was provided to parents while the kids engaged in thirty minutes of exertional exercise with a physical therapist, disguised as games. The final activity was preparing and eating healthy snacks. During class, children earned participation points that could be cashed in for age-appropriate prizes from a treasure chest at the end of the evening. After our last class, Nadine assured me that I was ready to implement the program independently at the community clinic.

I was grateful to be in the fellowship. I was being paid to have fun. I shopped for prizes, food, and even a treasure chest, and I was free to use my creativity to bring the program to life. It was as though I was seeing daylight for the first time in years. The tensions and never-ending demands of patient care that forced me into a life of tunnel vision at work had been lifted. Working twelve-hour night shifts, weekends, and holidays were on hold during the fellowship. I was giddy. I held my first class, which consisted of ten families, in the fall of 2007, after school, at a recreation center near the clinic. I was comfortable in this new role and looked forward to expanding the program to two locations, three to four times a year. The long-term plan was to offer classes at the clinic following the completion of the clinic expansion. Holding classes on-site would allow the clinic to bill insurance companies for patient visits, making the program more sustainable after my departure.

Wildfires Shut Down Clinic

A few weeks before my first KIDS class, a nearby wildfire caused all non-essential services across the county to be shut down for about a week. Hundreds of homes were lost in the fire, which created hazardous air quality. Mom and Grandpa Burt arrived from Minnesota that same week. The clinic closed due to dangerous air quality, so I had time off to visit with them. I cooked a turkey dinner, Mom's favorite, on the night of their arrival.

Upon arriving, Mom parked herself in front of the TV, and Grandpa Burt took a nap. His seventy-four-year-old body was exhausted after driving for twelve hours. Steve hadn't arrived home from work yet, and I was in the kitchen preparing dinner. "Hey Mom, Mom," I shouted from the kitchen over the noise of the TV, "why don't you come in here, where we can visit?"

Her reply caught me off guard, as I had forgotten our mother-daughter dynamics. I was the grown-up responsible one, and my mom was the distant, unengaged one in the relationship, leaving me in charge of everything. Clueless as to my emotions and motivation, she replied, "I'm going to watch the news, Debra."

It was a difficult and eye-opening week. Mom's last visit was before Don died, in our old house. Gradually, some of the old, familiar discomforts returned, such as not feeling understood and not understanding her own feelings. Despite our differences, I knew she loved me, and that was why she was visiting, so I focused on the positive and made their stay comfortable.

After dinner, we offered our recliners to Grandpa Burt and Mom and watched TV. I noticed my mother wasn't following anything on our favorite comedy show, so I offered to clarify the punch lines. I wondered if she was bored. "Mom, what do you usually like to watch when you're at home?"

"*Judge Judy* will be on soon, and after that, *Jeopardy*," she said, looking a little relieved.

By the end of the week, I was grateful for three things: the fire was extinguished, which meant the air quality had improved; our parents had left for home; and I was going to start my first KIDS class in a few days.

The two biggest challenges in keeping KIDS alive at the clinic were recruiting families with overweight children to participate and then offering the program in Spanish. Personnel from the Parks and Recreation Department and local school nurses assisted me in recruiting families from the surrounding low-income and Spanish-speaking neighborhoods. I offered nurses continuing education units for attending the program orientation and a training session. They were trained to identify overweight children who were heavier than 80 percent of children their same age and gender, according to standardized graphs commonly used in pediatrics. Physicians from the community clinic also referred families into the program.

For every English-speaking family that applied to KIDS, three Spanish-speaking families applied. I needed to motivate Spanish-speaking persons interested in combating childhood obesity to volunteer to teach KIDS in Spanish. I found volunteers through a local college's kinesiology and nutrition program. I arranged for the university to offer Spanish-fluent students an internship with college credits for teaching in the KIDS program. A formal agreement was secured between the school and the clinic. The college students shadowed Nadine, like I had, one night a week, and the next week, they and I taught the class to the Spanish-speaking families.

VA Homeless Shelter

An unexpected and gratifying experience in the fellowship was being assigned to visit men at the veterans' homeless shelter three mornings a week through the winter, and to arrange referrals to the Veterans Administration's hospital or clinic if necessary. I showed up in the dark, shortly before sunrise in November. It took a while to find a parking space, and the large canvas tent which was surrounded by chain-link fencing. I was warmly greeted by the person in charge, who directed me to a well-worn folding table and chair. Men were returning from nearby portable showers and preparing for the day. After breakfast, they would not be able to return to the shelter until dinner time. The scent of coffee and sausages drew me to rows of tables and chairs being wiped down by an assigned cleanup crew. Morning announcements could be heard in the background, reminding men to complete their assigned tasks and show up no later than 8:00 p.m. or they would not be readmitted.

As the greeter walked me to my station, he said, "If any of the men want to talk to you, they will look for you at this table; it's the health desk. As far as I know, no one was sick last night. You're not allowed anywhere else in the shelter. The men know they are to be respectful of you."

I spent an hour at the table, said "hi" to a few guys, and left thinking I needed to be doing something more. The remaining days, I arrived with an electric blood pressure monitor and offered blood pressure checks. Nurses are taught that the 'therapeutic use of self' is often more valuable than medications or procedures. This proved true at the shelter. The blood pressure readings were my way of saying, "You can approach me."

From there, I made small talk, asking, "Where are you from, or were you here last year?"

The men were self-sufficient and managed their own medications. Two of the residents will always be in my heart. Their honesty and vulnerability in trusting me with their stories about shame and regret humbled me, as did their heartfelt expression of gratitude for my listening presence on those cold mornings.

FELLOWSHIP EXTENSION 2008

I contacted my assistant department administrator (ADA) in orthopedics to request vacation time for the following year, anticipating that my temporary assignment would end in June. Her response went something like this:

"I'm not sure what to say about your vacation request, Debbie. We can't take you back. We're having budget problems; you will have to see about extending the fellowship. Oh, by the way, The Trauma Team won the Team Excellence Award; since you nominated them, you're invited to attend the ceremony."

I wasn't surprised by her response or the award. Since I was just getting started at the clinic, I could easily keep myself busy for another year. "Okay, I'll let the fellowship director know. It's up to her, I guess."

At the conclusion of that call, my mind began racing with what-ifs and what's next thoughts. The truth was that I was replaceable and there was no guarantee I'd ever get my job back. I was a one-trick pony; orthopedics was all I knew. I hated the thought of starting over at age fifty. I would have to reinvent myself as a nurse practitioner if I were going to keep working, and I needed to work for my retirement benefits, the income, and my sanity. I obsessed over the idea that if I didn't get back to this position, I might lose my pension. I remained at the clinic until 2010 and in the fellowship until August of 2011. I continued to apply for positions with my employer, hoping to keep my seniority and benefits. All email and phone communication with members of the orthopedic department stopped in the second year of the fellowship, when my ADA transferred to a new department. Once, while dining at a restaurant with my husband, I was completely ignored by a nearby table of orthopedic surgeons with whom I had worked. It was obvious that they recognized me, yet they didn't acknowledge my presence. Another awkward moment was when I realized that the orthopedic department was having a staff meeting in the classroom next to my NAON meeting. While waiting in the hall during a break, a PA from Ortho started to talk with me, but cut herself short, telling me she didn't want the new manager to see her talking with me. I was now a complete outsider, and I didn't know why.

Ancillary Clinic Duties

Despite not being accepted into a PhD public health program, the fellowship provided many opportunities to participate in the local public health community. Dr. Kat, the medical director, appointed me to be a clinic representative in the community on several occasions. I served on a task force to improve access to orthopedic services and was a member of the county Childhood Obesity Action Network. I participated in a collaboration of community leaders, which included the director of the Nurse Family Partnership (NFP). She invited me to serve as an adviser and to recruit program participants. Their goals were to improve pregnancy outcomes, enhance child health, and assist low-income first-time moms to become more economically self-sufficient. My connections with the clinic and local school nurses helped me recruit pregnant moms into the program. My personal history as a teenage mother and my experience as an NP student in the pregnant minor program served me well in the advising role.

STARTING MY FIRST DOCTORATE PROGRAM

Having a consistent day of the week guaranteed off for the first time in over twenty years added flexibility, allowing me to enroll in a Doctor of Nursing Practice (DNP) program at a local state university. Classes met on my day off from the clinic. Completing the DNP program was the first of many challenging steps in reinventing myself as an NP. However, returning to the classroom was difficult, especially learning new computer skills for researching databases, designing presentations, registering for classes, and managing homework assignments. Additionally, I didn't know how to type. I truly felt like a fish out of water, or maybe a dinosaur.

The DNP degree was designed as an advanced clinical degree, with the possibility of applying required clinical hours toward a specialty, such as orthopedics. Courses beyond the master's degree included advanced pathogenesis of complex disease, health informatics, health policy, healthcare financing, and evidence-based practice research. I loved learning everything, but hated the aggravation of learning to use technology.

I graduated from the DNP program before departing from the community clinic. My final project was developing a program plan and evaluation for the KIDS program. I presented my outcome statistics to the clinic director, Dr. Kat, and my faculty advisor the week before leaving the clinic.

Additional projects completed during the fellowship that contributed to the DNP requirements included writing the "Musculoskeletal

Examination" chapter for the *NAON Core Curriculum for Orthopedic Nursing, 7th ed.*, and collaborating as the NAON chapter leader with several other nursing specialty organizations to provide nursing education programs for nurses in Southern California. During these professional opportunities, I learned from nursing colleagues the value of networking and sharing our gifts and talents for the greater good of our profession and the patients we serve. Proceeds from the education programs were used to fund the establishment of two new local nursing chapters: one for the National Association of Orthopedic Nurses (NAON) and the other for the California Association for Nurse Practitioners (CANP).

LEAVING THE COMMUNITY CLINIC

Departing from the community clinic was a bittersweet experience. The experience was a gift and a blessing professionally, academically, and personally. I was introduced to the reality of healthcare outside of my comfort zone, in a clinic where I was the minority and an outsider, which was a humbling experience. I learned to earn the trust of the Spanish-speaking medical assistants and staff at the clinic. I also recognized the vast inequities between the community clinics' patient population and the more affluent populations, which have greater access to care and resources. Learning about the latest advances in diabetes and hypertension care and leadership experiences were also benefits from the fellowship, which would serve me well in my next career pursuits. My greatest opportunity for reinventing myself professionally was the flexibility in my schedule created by those who collaborated behind the scenes in creating the fellowship, the gift of time, and shared resources.

Dr. Kat arranged our final meeting after my last DNP class. We met in the shabby office we had shared for three years. Dressed in comfortable, casual slacks and a button-down blouse with her hair in a ponytail, she looked at me and said, "Debbie, it's time for you to spread your wings and fly. I am sorry to inform you that the administration has decided to no longer participate in the fellowship arrangement. I wish you the best wherever you go."

I peered into her kind face as she spoke the words, nodding my head in acknowledgment, a little too choked up to speak. I knew the day would come, but I wasn't prepared.

Dr. Kat was a mentor in grace and persistence, and generous in extending the fellowship beyond year one while I honed my leadership skills and completed my doctorate degree. The clinic more than honored their agreement in offering a fellowship. However, my employer's intentions regarding my future in the organization were uncertain.

LIMBO BEGINS: 2010-2011

The Fellowship director continued to fund my efforts in improving access to orthopedic care in the community when she learned that the orthopedic department was not taking me back. I was grateful for her support. My goal was to implement an orthopedic NP residency program at the university and find an orthopedic practice willing to provide experienced DNP students with orthopedic experience. I presented a proposal to the university and secured a surgeon partner at a private orthopedic practice.

While waiting for the university's response to my proposal, I changed direction, realizing my plan had limitations. The university and I were not officially connected to an academic orthopedic institution, the necessary supplier of surgeon mentors over time, and I didn't have the support of my previous orthopedic employer. Therefore, I had no standing in the orthopedic community despite my experience and credentials. I discovered my old ADA had returned to orthopedics as their department administrator (DA), and I hoped that she would convince the new chief to reassign me to my former position, relieving me of my temporary assignment.

After four years on temporary assignment, I returned to the Orthopedic department and was scheduled for new hire orientation, followed by placement on probation. PA Mike was assigned to oversee my orientation and schedule my assignments. I went along with the plan with substantial reservations. Frankly, I didn't trust him. He had advertised and recruited through a physician assistant website for new PAs for the department to replace me, knowing I was trying to get my job back. Five new PAs were hired during my four-year absence. He had a bias in favor of PAs, and I had a reason to fear I might not make it to full retirement.

OCTOBER 2011, 9:00 A.M.

ORTHOPEDIC DEPARTMENT

I approached the new medical director's closed office door, knocked, and waited for an invitation to enter. I was nervous, unsure of the reason for this second performance evaluation in less than a month. Dr. D started the meeting with a summary statement indicating concerns raised by a few of the physicians about my ability to continue in the department, along with alleged patient complaints, shoddy documentation, and tardiness. I listened tentatively, perplexed and concerned, as the allegations were new to me, except for the day I was ten minutes late. As we discussed each point, I respectfully addressed each one, providing context and evidence that countered his claims. After my previous meeting with Dr. D, I anticipated needing objective evidence of my performance for my next evaluation, so I asked each doctor I worked with to evaluate my performance on a brief survey I had crafted, which included room for comments. The consensus was that my patient care and charting were appropriate and without any deficiencies. I came prepared to defend my work, but I was unprepared for the dismissive response and the order to cease "pestering the doctors," as I was making them feel uncomfortable. I knew my electronic charting was slow and I was a bit rusty, but I also knew patient care had never suffered.

HOSPITAL EMERGENCY ROOM, FIVE WEEKS LATER

It all came to a head in the emergency room. Dr. D had ordered that, as a condition of my continued employment, an overseer be assigned to evaluate my performance in seeing patients. I felt humiliated and confused.

Then one day in the emergency room, I was being observed by a newly hired and significantly less experienced PA. During an examination of an elderly woman with a hip fracture, he asked questions I thought he should have known the answers to. That is when I recognized the significant gap between us in both years of experience and knowledge. This triggered in me a sense of outrage, followed by intense emotional conflict driven by sadness and anger. In that moment, I finally fully realized that they did not want me. My twenty-plus years of outstanding evaluations didn't matter. My work in the department didn't matter. My perceived past friendships with those left in the department didn't matter. My love and emotional attachment to the department didn't matter. They wanted me out, and it was over. I felt as though a scar had been ripped open, revealing my inner woundedness, draining life-sustaining fluids from my body, as the uncomfortable truth surfaced from deep within. Subconscious childhood wounds caused by fear and betrayal were exposed. Damaged trust issues, which I had managed to keep under control until that moment, erupted into sadness and anger. I felt lightheaded. I felt out of control. I needed help. Without conscious understanding, my internal self-preservation mode kicked in and enabled me to finish writing hospital admission and preoperative surgical orders for the frail woman in our care.

Feeling confident that our patient was stable and ready for transfer to the orthopedic ward, I exited the ER and quickly entered the nearest private office. I felt a pounding in my chest as I placed a phone call and waited to hear a voice from the other end. Time seemed to slow down between rings. The moisture in my mouth evaporated as perspiration slipped from my armpits, wetting the well-worn white lab coat embroidered with the name Debra Palmer, Family Nurse Practitioner. I unconsciously gripped the phone handle with the same intensity as the neck tension I'd been feeling for the past month.

In a magical moment of heightened awareness, my thoughts connected to the physical sensations in my body and identified the emotional roller coaster I was experiencing. Fear, anger, and mistrust were competing for my attention. The same suppressed emotions I denied for the past two months could no longer be contained. Instinctively, I recognized I needed help and made the equivalent of a 911 distress call; I made a cry for help to the Employee Relations Office. They had previously resolved an issue for me, and I trusted them. At that moment, I didn't trust myself or my team members in the orthopedic department. "God help me," I whispered under my breath, waiting for someone to pick up as the phone continued to ring for what seemed like several minutes.

The calm, soothing voice of the woman who answered was worth waiting for. I struggled to articulate words with what seemed like a thick cotton tongue. She listened patiently, allowing me to unload my frustrations and anxiety without interrupting me. When I ran out of words, she slowly asked me a series of questions in a measured rhythm. The one question I'll never forget was: "Is anyone at risk of being harmed or potentially in danger?"

To my astonishment, I immediately yelled into the phone, "Yes! Absolutely! My patients are."

Once that revelation sank in, I slowed my speech and explained, "I just don't trust my judgment right now. I'm not thinking straight. I'm afraid of making a mistake, like a drug error or missing an important test result. I'm not myself, and I feel like I'm jumping out of my skin! I don't know what to do!"

A hot tear trickled down my cheek as I realized how vulnerable I had become and how out of control I felt. She asked me more questions and calmly provided a series of instructions that I was told to write down and share with my supervisor.

I hung up the phone, shaking in disbelief at what had just happened in a three-minute call. I was instructed to tell my supervisor I was dismissed for the day and would not be returning for a minimum of two weeks. I was scheduled to report at 9:00 a.m. the next day to a given address. Even though the PA evaluating me that day took over my responsibilities, my heart was burdened with guilt and shame for having to leave in the middle of my shift. I felt as though I was abandoning my team and my patient. As I walked towards my car, I felt a huge weight lifting from my shoulders as I replayed the phone call in my mind. The woman on the phone seemed to grasp my concerns. A sense of calm overcame me as though I had just escaped a life-threatening storm. However, the storm was not over. Shame and guilt did not lift. Instead, they embraced me like the hot, heavy, sticky air that follows a tropical storm. In that moment, haunting memories of shame and guilt took over my thoughts.

I climbed into my Honda Civic, buckled in, and paused as heartache and thoughts of lament from my childhood occupied my mind, taking me back to 1971 in Duluth, Minnesota, the day my fears, distrust, and feelings of betrayal drove me to abandon my mother and siblings, creating in me a sense of shame and guilt. The feelings that I had hidden deep within for so long were resurfacing.

My trusted team leaders had retired, and the orthopedic family I had grown to love and trust no longer existed, except in my mind. Why that decision? Perhaps they thought I had abandoned and rejected them, or they preferred PAs, or it could have been a budget decision; I was the most expensive NP in the department with maximum vacation and sick time benefits. Regardless, my potential dismissal triggered feelings of betrayal, evoking the familiar feelings of mistrust and abandonment from my youth. Not wanting to face the painful truth, I had ignored all the signs. Recognizing my vulnerable and fragile state, I was enrolled in an employer-offered program, "Back to Work," for individuals experiencing difficult transitions. While I was in the program, the manager of a clinic I had applied to work at contacted me. She was a friend of Jane, my friend from HAC. "Debbie, I would love to hire you, but I can't since your last credential expired in 2008."

I was shocked. I knew I had resubmitted credentialing paperwork in 2010. Apparently, the chief never signed off on them. Without credentials, I was not eligible for any position within the organization, and without recent orthopedic experience, no orthopedic department outside the organization would hire me. This realization reaffirmed my suspicions; they never planned to take me back. Let me be clear: my telling of this part of my life is not to assess fault or blame. In fact, it's an excellent HMO with a top-notch orthopedic department. What I am saying is that I was blind to the reality of what was happening, and what happened was exceedingly painful, triggering strong emotions rising from my past.

Counseling

With a reluctant and heavy heart, I secured the counseling services of Dr. Thomas, a plump woman in her sixties with short curly grey hair and a PhD in psychology. A friend from the Guatemala Project recommended her. After a few months, Dr. Thomas shared her concerns with me. "I believe you are experiencing anxiety and post-traumatic stress," she explained.

I was surprised at her PTSD assessment. "Really? What gives you that impression?" I asked, trying to make sense of her diagnosis.

"I think you will agree. You've had sleep disturbance, nightmares, and insomnia, right?" I nodded. "You've described frequently feeling on edge and a loss of interest in pleasurable activities. Last month, you canceled plans to attend an out-of-town birthday celebration you had been looking forward to."

She continued listing evidence supporting her concerns until I interrupted, "I see what you mean, maybe you're right," I mumbled as I stared out the window.

Following our discussion, she extended my disability, scheduled another appointment, and referred me to a psychiatrist for medication management of anxiety and insomnia. I met with the psychiatrist a few weeks later.

"Mrs. Palmer, it's not uncommon to be on this medication for at least nine months to a year, or longer."

I nodded in acknowledgement, trying to hide my horror. I promised myself I'd be off the antidepressants in six months.

After a few weeks on the medications, I noticed an improvement in sleep quality and suppression of my frequent racing thoughts. Life resumed, but in slow motion. I went from less than five to ten hours of sleep at night. Feeling out of it, I cut my dose in half. I continued volunteer work as the new CANP chapter president and state health policy chair, but turned over the reins of the NAON chapter to Michelle, the new president. On the way home from a CANP meeting, an NP colleague who carpooled with me that evening shared an observation that astonished me: "You were great tonight, better than I've ever seen you. More focused, and not in a hurry."

She knew me from the community clinic. We had carpooled often, so she knew me well enough to know something was different. In an instant, I knew it was the medication, but there was no way I'd tell her that. I was uncomfortable with the truth.

My sleep improved along with my mood and optimism, and my positive thinking returned. I began each day with meditation and prayer, feeling less anxious and more hopeful about my future. I rearranged my finances to accommodate an anticipated drop in income, and I took a long-overdue vacation to Paris with Steve and Michelle. The time away was a healing balm. I took stock in my blessings and friendships, trying to focus on positive things and letting go of bitterness and feelings of betrayal. Four friends from my past, also struggling with unexpected job loss, became my unofficial support system.

Stage Two Reflections: Acknowledging our Oneness

Just as stage-two wound healing requires the elimination of harmful debris and organisms from the wound site, I had to end the harmful belief that my value and worth were dependent on being an ONP and end my unhealthy employment relationships, which hindered my well-being. Like inflammation, the process was heated and painful. Developing healthy boundaries, seeking personal and professional support services, and a commitment to lifelong learning experiences taught me to trust my inner voice, the one that warned me when temperatures and pressures were rising to dangerous levels, and how to discern help from harm.

Stage two emotional spiritual healing required acknowledging our oneness or universal inclusivity, a belief that we are all part of one human family equally valued by the creator, connected with the Divine Creator and one another, through the universal experiences of living and dying amid wounds, suffering, and healing.

PART THREE
BUILDING

PROLIFERATION

Repairing and rebuilding destroyed, missing, and damaged tissue begins as blood vessels proliferate at the wound base to transport oxygen and nutrients necessary for producing new tissue to cover the wound, bridging the gap. This crucial stage strengthens the damaged area in preparation for the final healing stage.

CHAPTER NINE

OPEN ACCESS

Recently, I told my fourteen-year-old granddaughter that the only good thing that happened to me in 2011 was her birth. As I put words on this page, I realized I was wrong. I was focusing on my losses, rather than the gains and abundance I experienced by the year's end. Grandpa Burt died of cancer in the spring, and Mom began drowning her sadness with alcohol. My pain was accentuated with the loss of my orthopedic position and associated feelings of betrayal and rejection. What I did not recall in my conversation with my granddaughter was the gift of a friend and colleague who entered my life . . . once again unexpectedly. Like an angel, she showed up and had my back.

NP KATE

I was introduced to Dr. Todd, an associate dean of a Christian university, at the third annual Doctorate in Nursing Practice (DNP) conference. Kate, my first NP preceptor, orchestrated the informal and impromptu meeting. Coincidentally, Dr. Todd saw me present earlier in the day on a panel presentation about DNP orthopedic residencies.

Later that evening, Kate called me. Her new position on a faculty search committee, where Dr. Todd worked, prompted the call. Our conversation went something like this:

"I've recommended you for a teaching position at the university where Dr. Todd works. They need doctorally prepared faculty to teach in their new NP program, and I think you'd be a good fit. Their hiring process is lengthy. Applications for next fall's faculty positions are currently being accepted. They only hire professed Christians. If you're interested, I suggest you send me your CV for review before applying for a position starting next fall. I can coach you up to the time of the interview. After that, you're on your own."

The application process was indeed lengthy! By spring, I had five interviews and presented to the nursing faculty at their monthly meeting. I spoke for about forty minutes following three other aspiring faculty members. My KIDS presentation was followed by a lively Q&A session leading up to lunch.

As I concluded the presentation, I noticed my audience for the first time that morning: a large, diverse group of approximately 200 nursing faculty. Men and women of all ages and ethnicities asked thoughtful questions. I shared some of the problems I encountered while collecting survey results, the mistakes that were made, and my shock in learning that the average education level of parents in my first few classes was third grade, in Mexico; a finding I wished I had discovered before starting the classes, not three years later when tallying up my results for my final DNP presentation. A few months later, I accepted an assistant professor of nursing position for the 2012-13 academic year. I also submitted my resignation to the HMO, as I had exhausted the last of my accrued vacation and sick time to qualify for retirement benefits.

Parenting: Does It Ever End?

January 2012

On a gloomy Saturday morning, we knocked on our twenty-one-year-old son's bedroom door. He was slow to rouse, but we persisted. Steve took the lead in starting the conversation.

"Garrett, we agreed you could live at home if you were working or going to school, and right now, you're not doing either. We're happy to reimburse you for your tuition and books if you return to school and maintain a B average; however, we will no longer cover the cost of classes that you fail or drop out of."

We gave him a three-month deadline until April 1st to either find a job, start school, or move out. It was a difficult decision, and we would have made it sooner, but Steve felt we were responsible for him until he was a legal consenting adult.

April 1, 2012

"Knock, knock, it's moving day!"

"What are you talking about?" Garrett asked as he pulled himself out of slumberland.

"We've been warning you. We were serious."

"I don't remember you giving me a specific date. Is this an April Fool's Day joke?"

"It isn't a joke. We've rented a room for you and purchased a bus pass to help you get around while job hunting. We have been trying to prepare you for it," I told him.

Garrett stayed in the boarding house for a month. While living in the boarding house, he enjoyed visiting with the retired seniors in the lobby and playing the piano for them. He shared with me a conversation he had with one of the seniors that prompted his move.

"Why are you living here? You don't look like a drug addict, you seem like a nice young man, you don't belong here," the man had said to him.

The following month, he moved north to work for his brother.

I stayed in contact with Garrett during his transition, maintaining clear expectations and open communication regarding our agreements. This put him in charge of his future. Eventually, he sold his clarinet to pay for tuition at a community college, moved back home, and graduated with an Associate of Arts Degree three years later, when he applied for transfer to a four-year university. Of the five schools that accepted him, he chose the University of California, Los Angeles (UCLA). I disagreed with his choice, but I accepted it. I thought it would be better to attend a college closer to home. Building a parental relationship with him as an adult was a new and challenging experience that began with this baby step of recognizing his autonomy and being supportive.

Depression Follow-Up

The month I accepted a faculty position, I stopped taking antidepressants, hopeful and confident, yet realistic about my limitations. Kate's coaching helped me during the application process. I spent the summer studying textbooks and shadowing summer school faculty as I prepared to teach the fall semester's Advanced Health Assessment course and precept students at a homeless healthcare clinic two days a week.

I met Lydia, a friendly NP, at the all-faculty orientation on the main campus. We shared our teaching loads with one another over lunch. She had once taught Health Assessment on another campus.

"I know how nerve-wracking it can be in your first semester. Do you have the slides that go with the textbook for teaching the course?"

"No, I didn't know there was such a thing. Do you know how I can get them?" I asked.

"I'll connect you with someone who can help," she said with a nod and an assuring smile as she stood up to toss her paper plate. I seldom missed the chance to connect with her at monthly meetings after that.

The kick-off for the new school year, welcoming new and returning faculty, was like attending a megachurch worship service. It was held at the main campus, a few hours away. As I entered the auditorium, the pounding beat of drums in the band welcomed me in. They were playing my favorite songs from K-LOVE Christian radio. An inspiring message, like a sermon, was followed by prayers of encouragement to do God's work, teaching with love. I left feeling renewed and optimistic.

SIMULATION LABS

Being assigned to create simulation experiences to evaluate students in Health Assessment was wholly unexpected. I was unprepared; I didn't even know what a simulation was.

The university had just completed a state-of-the-art nursing lab that mirrored real-life clinic examination rooms for simulation experiences. Professional patients, hired by the university to follow a script with students in the lab, replaced evaluations with actual patient visits in the clinic. I found the experience to be superior to evaluating students in less controlled clinical experiences. It was also superior to my NP health assessment classroom thirty years earlier, when fellow students examined each other, including female gynecologic exams.

I approached my new assignment with curiosity and a little trepidation. Fortunately, I had the assistance of Carrie, an RN in her thirties, with experience in military simulation training. She trained me to develop scripts for simulations, evaluate student performance, and run a simulation lab. She shared a useful framework to ensure that students include all relevant body systems in formulating a diagnosis, using the mnemonic VINDICATE. I wish I had known about this simple tool years earlier. I implemented this framework when teaching, using it as a learning tool. The supportive VINDICATE tool was designed to prompt thoughts that may help avoid missing possible underlying causes of patient symptoms and inform a diagnosis.

VASCULAR

INFECTION

NEOPLASTIC

DEGENERATIVE

IATROGENIC/INTOXICATION

CONGENITAL

AUTOIMMUNE

TRAUMA

ENDOCRINE/METABOLIC

Faculty from all campuses collaborated in developing evidence-based simulation scripts and rubrics for evaluating simulation experiences and shared them across all campuses.

LEARNING WITH MY STUDENTS

The university implemented an RN to BSN Program in response to the rising demand by hospitals for bachelor's degree-prepared RNs. I was assigned to teach pathophysiology, the study of how abnormal physiology leads to disease, to the RN students. The faculty version of the textbook included epigenetics, information new to me. Epigenetics is the study of changes in genetic activity and their effects on future generations, acquired modifications in the body influencing the body's development, and the risk of disease. Included in epigenetics is the study of external factors in the environment, lifestyles, and individual experiences influencing changes in the body. What I shared with my students was how our genetic makeup can be altered before conception, within our mother's uterus, or after we are born through the process of epigenetics. According to several studies, [11, 12, 13] many environmental and social experiences are linked to the alteration of genetics. I wondered about the effects of traumatic experiences influencing inherited genetic code in myself, my offspring, and my brother Paul's condition since birth. Could it explain the generations of OCD and alcoholism in my family?

Just as the expansion of new blood vessels increases the flow of nutrients to heal a wound, advancements in scientific evidence and technology over time contribute to our understanding of physical and emotional healing.

Teaching 2013

The dreaded two-hour drive, carpooling to monthly faculty meetings, provided an opportunity to meet and network with fellow faculty members across regions. In January, I opened the meeting with a Bible verse and a devotion. As a new professor of nursing, I was a little intimidated in the presence of my fellow scholars. Standing at the podium, a little nervous, I spoke into the microphone.

"Today's scripture reading is from my favorite New Testament verse, Philippians chapter four verse thirteen: 'I can do all things through Christ who strengthens me.'"

I asked the group to recall their first teaching assignment and shared how I embraced the message three months prior in my first course as a faculty member. I asked them to consider future challenges and envision positive outcomes for those challenges. Next, I reminded them of their prior positive teaching experience and the affirmation in that day's verse that I hoped would encourage and inspire them in future challenges.

In preparing for the meeting, I considered the verse's application in my own life. My children have called me the "Worst Case Scenario Mom" since their teen years. They were correct in their assessment of me. My decisions were often based on fear of the worst possible outcomes. I convinced myself that the fears were rational and necessary for keeping my family and patients safe. Over time, the root of the concern and rationale for my pessimism emerged. Having parents with mental illness and alcoholism taught me to expect the worst and hope for the best by preparing for the worst possible outcome. Unfortunately, this motto paralyzed me as much as it motivated me.

PhD and Me

Following that January meeting, I faced my fear of failing and embraced Philippians 4:13 when applying to a PhD program. It was a bold choice. Taking on new challenges in the infancy of my teaching career was risky. Overextending my financial, emotional, and physical resources could result in compromises or failures at home, work, or in the program. However, success was also possible. I refused to allow self-doubt and fear of failure to dictate my decision, nor the belief that I was too old, as I'd be the same age in four years, with or without a PhD. I hoped that completing a PhD would increase my knowledge, skills, and opportunities for professional advancement, leading to a pay increase.

I was accepted into a DNP to PhD bridge program, where three classes from my DNP program were transferred toward PhD graduation requirements. Tuition was covered through the Nurse Faculty Loan Program (NFLP), which was eighty percent forgivable after five years of full-time teaching. I anticipated graduation in 2017. I did not expect the loss of valuable support from my original cohorts when I advanced a year ahead of them as a student in the Bridge program. I missed the camaraderie we built during my first year, sharing resources, collaborating, and working as a team on class presentations, and I'd miss celebrating graduation with them.

San Francisco 2013 CANP Annual Meeting

In the spring of 2013, Michael and my two-year-old granddaughter looked on as the CANP awarded me their Bridging Health Care

Needs Award. Nick, an NP who volunteered with me on two medical missions, introduced me. I listened with appreciation as comments from my peers were read aloud about my mission work in Guatemala and efforts to increase access to specialty orthopedic care.

As an inaugural chapter president, health policy chair, and CANP member, I was proud to be part of this organization, which underwent significant transformation and strengthening during my tenure with the board of directors. For the first time in its thirty-year history, over thirty separate, unaffiliated chapters with distinctly different bylaws united under one set of bylaws and a single website. This enabled improved open lines of communication between chapter members, leaders, and the leadership board, unifying and strengthening the organization. The unified structure added necessary vitality and life for future organizational growth and interprofessional relationships. However, the unification of CANP came at a price. Just as sutures stitch together a wound, creating tension while bringing edges together, the commitment of members to sit in tense moments, experiencing tension over time as they made a more unified and stronger organization, was necessary. Successful unification came in the process of pulling all sides into alignment, unifying the edges as one entity, like healing a stitched wound.

Before the start of the PhD program, I enrolled in a three-unit nurse educator course to fulfill a nurse faculty loan requirement. The professor, Dr. Georges, taught philosophy in my DNP program. Her course was instrumental in rebuilding my confidence as an NP while struggling to redefine myself as an NP during the fellowship program. Her compassion and honesty in difficult conversations were healing to me, as was her assignment to "Define your philosophy of nursing."

That assignment forced me to examine my values, beliefs, and personal philosophy as a nurse and contributed to my decision to author this book. I worked harder on that paper than on any other assignment that year, even though we were all promised an A no matter what we turned in. Her teaching style was somewhat unconventional, allowing students to direct their own growth. The course and its required reading, *Educating Nurses: A Call for Radical Transformation*, had a profoundly positive effect on me as a faculty member entering my second year of teaching. It brought me back to my origins as an RN student, reminding me of core principles and methods for educating all nurses.

REFLECTIONS

My orthopedic career ended, but my self-esteem and confidence as a nurse practitioner remained intact. Returning to school, working in the community clinic, and making the most of the fellowship experience strengthened and reinforced my NP foundation and provided building blocks for rebuilding my personal and professional life. Just as open blood vessels transport healing elements, I had to stay open-minded to the potential benefits of new experiences, opportunities, and new scientific knowledge to avoid obstructing my healing path with negative thoughts and attitudes.

CHAPTER TEN

STRONGER SUPPORT STRUCTURES

At the end of my first teaching semester, I received average to mediocre evaluations from my students. Their honest critique was humbling. I was grateful for the honesty of the student who pointed out my tendency to talk over others in class. She was right, and I was embarrassed by the revelation. Student input heavily influenced faculty evaluations: I needed to improve and vowed to be more like my DNP faculty. I tried emulating those who connected well with students by first noting our differences in teaching styles. My style was more abrupt in delivering a lecture, while my teachers were more interactive. Conscious efforts to be more interactive and offer positive feedback before delivering constructive criticism improved communication with my students and ultimately enhanced my future performance evaluations.

I didn't know what I'd been missing until my second year of teaching, when Gayle, an experienced NP educator, was hired as my new on-site director. Knowing I was new to academics, she sat in the back of my class and shared her perspective on my teaching. Her feedback was helpful, encouraging, and assuring. She also invited me to observe in her classroom. I was impressed by her command of the classroom and her intuition in knowing when to pause, clarify, and include students in the experience. Having had her supportive positive influence in the office next to mine, and not seventy-five miles away, provided the oxygen and nutrients I needed for repairing my damaged confidence and fueling my growth as faculty.

Teaching Role Development

Role Development was my favorite class to teach. Weekly, I introduced the class to new NPs, nurse midwives, anesthetists, and clinical specialists to inspire them on their NP journey. I was relentless in reaching out to NP friends, former work colleagues, fellow faculty, professors in my PhD program, and members of CANP and asking them to share their work experiences with my students. Recruiting speakers was time-intensive; however, once they volunteered, most returned or referred me to other NPs for future semesters. Interactions between students and guest speakers fueled honest dialogue regarding job preparation, employer expectations, and work-life balance. Additionally, questions surfaced about work sites and collegial relationships with physicians. The differences between shared work experiences were remarkable, especially between federally funded community clinics for low-income patients and private practice clinics, unionized and non-union settings, and generalist versus specialist NP roles. The guest speakers exposed students to a multitude of settings and roles, offering them the most essential building block: hope and a glimpse of what was possible beyond graduation.

Occasionally, guest speakers offered to precept students at their clinic sites. One stands out in my memory in part because of her amazing NP Journey. Autumn was a medical assistant under Dr. Charles when I first joined the orthopedics department. As a full-time married employee with a child, she methodically climbed the nursing education ladder, first as a medical assistant, followed by LPN and RN training, and most recently, a nurse practitioner program. After years of working together in the Thursday evening fracture clinic, our friendship grew. We celebrated our daughter's birthdays, the graduations of colleagues who advanced the nursing ladder, and those who retired. We also shared in grieving the loss of our beloved colleagues, especially Dr. Charles. At the end of her first visit to my Nursing Role class, she shared a piece of advice, something she attributed to me. "When school gets hard, picture yourself wearing a cap and gown on graduation day, walking down the aisle to the organ music of pomp and circumstance. And remind yourself that you are working towards that day, tell yourself to keep going, you can do it, it's all about delayed gratification and becoming what you believe is possible."

To meet course requirements, I asked guest speakers to share how they integrated core NP competencies: direct patient care, coaching, collaboration, consultation, research, leadership, advocacy, and ethical decision making into their practice. My students benefited from their answers. My most excellent external resource in teaching Role was my authentic and supportive network of colleagues in the community. Years of building long-term professional relationships enabled me to provide meaningful classroom experiences and enhanced my sense of belonging in my profession. During my tenure teaching the Role course, our student scores in the professional development section of the national NP certification exam increased, along with my own self-confidence and enthusiasm as a faculty member.

Entering the PhD program early in my new teaching career required confidence, dedication, and funding. Reminding myself of the successful strategies I learned in the DNP program, along with Steve's support and confidence, boosted my own confidence. Having the Nurse Faculty Loan and encouragement from fellow PhD colleagues and friends added to that boost. More importantly, my plan was in alignment with my new purpose. No longer a clinician, I would become the best nursing professor I could be by relying on my higher power, the Creator, to guide and strengthen me in the process. Gayle arranged my teaching schedule around PhD classes, and fellow faculty served as my cheerleading squad, offering suggestions and sharing examples of how they got through their programs.

JOY

Peggy was an unexpected source of encouragement and inspiration during the PhD program. We met when our children were in a youth group in the JOY Bible Study class, composed of parents of kids in the church youth group. After ten years, the group dwindled to three couples. We met monthly, rotating between homes to share a meal and discuss a Christian-based book. Peggy, one of the members, was in a PhD program. During the Christmas break of 2014, we met in her home. After dinner, the men wandered off to talk football while Peg and I compared PhD experiences. She had university support for tuition and a monthly stipend, so she did not have to work while in school. We both planned to do qualitative research, collecting non-numerical information like interview transcripts, observations, and answers to open-ended questions. Information would be analyzed to discover patterns, themes, and subjective perspectives about meanings and insights. I was amazed to hear the similarities and differences between our experiences. Peggy was a quiet, reserved type, not one to boast or brag. I marveled at her progress as she shared, "My chair wants me to publish the results of a study I did as an assignment in my quantitative methods class. I am going to submit it. It is the first step in moving forward with the research I want to do."

"So, when do you think you will have a research proposal ready to defend?" I asked.

In a neutral tone, she stated, "I have already defended my research proposal; next, I need approval from the institutional review board to proceed. I'm in the process of submitting my application."

I was happy for Peggy, but disappointed with my own progress. I had not yet narrowed down a research topic, let alone a research question. I was emotionally connected to studying childhood adversity, the topic of D. Felitti's research. My last contact with him was during the DNP program. I decided to reconnect with him for research ideas to build on his prior work.

Dr. Felitti invited me for lunch and met me in the dining room of the University Club, where he was on faculty. I was too nervous to eat, so I settled on iced tea. He had not changed much since our time in HAC. I started the conversation with, "Thank you for agreeing to meet with me again. As I mentioned on the phone, I'm in a PhD program. I finished the DNP program; my final manuscript was related to obesity, as we discussed when we last met. I could not return to orthopedics, so I entered the academic world. As you may know, many academic scholars believe the PhD is the terminal degree, not the clinical or professional doctorate degree. That is why I'm back in school. I need to narrow down my research topic. I was hoping you might have suggestions about the adverse childhood study."

He complimented my professional pursuits and updated me on additional studies related to his original study. At one point in our meeting, I asked, "What do you think accounts for the resilience of individuals with high ACE scores who do not develop chronic diseases?"

He answered me with a few stories about prior patients who appeared healthy with high ACE scores. The stories illustrated his belief that no one escapes the effects of toxic stress from childhood adversity. I wondered about my own ACE score of 9 out of 10 adversities.

At the end of our hour-long conversation, he suggested I connect with Casey Gwin, author of *Cheering for the Children*[14]. Before we parted, he agreed to keep me in mind if research opportunities appeared on his radar.

Eager to know more about Mr. Gwinn, I ordered his book for our meeting. I first met Mr. Gwinn as the founder of the Family Justice Center during my fellowship, so I immediately recognized him as I entered his office. He stood up as I entered and reached out to shake my hand. "Thank you for meeting with me," I said. "Dr. Felitti spoke highly of you and seemed to think you may have a research idea for me related to adverse childhood experiences."

He invited me to sit and gave me his full attention. We spoke for about thirty minutes, bouncing ideas back and forth related to his work studying the concept of hope held by victims of violence.

In the end, his leads did not result in a final research topic. However, our conversation and the premise of his book intrigued me. One adult, a neighbor, teacher, youth leader, or relative, connecting with a traumatized child in a meaningful way, may be the catalyst to building resilience and healing in a child overcoming adversity. As I left his office, I thought about the catalysts in my life who had aided in building my resilience in overcoming my own childhood challenges. I am forever grateful to all of them: teachers, school nurses, youth leaders, social workers, family members, and friends.

2014 Necessary Adjustments

After contemplating our future, Steve and I decided to simplify our lives and lower our expenses by downsizing into a smaller, newer home. My faculty pay was 50 percent less than what I earned in the HMO, and my self-imposed, never-ending list of do-it-yourself (DIY) home improvement projects had become too much of a distraction for me to resist. I was addicted to DIY projects; they provided both joy and distraction. Unfinished home improvement projects distracted me from working on my dissertation. We finished an outdoor project in time to celebrate our thirty-fifth wedding anniversary with a party on the patio before putting the house with the citrus trees and chicken-coop for sale.

Thirty-Fifth Anniversary

Our celebration was like a healing balm following years of struggles in both of our careers. Michael, his two daughters, and Michelle, now twenty-eight, traveled from Northern California to attend. Garrett was living at home and attending a community college. I was happy to have all of them home together. My aunts from Minnesota, now in their seventies, came and enthusiastically decorated the patio and directed traffic to an empty nearby lot. Steve's sister traveled from Las Vegas with her spouse, and cousins and uncles came. Musician friends soothed our souls with poolside tunes, and a New Orleans-style food truck served Mardi Gras food complete with beignets. My dear friend Jennie, a licensed pastor since our mission trip to Guatemala, performed a short service as we renewed our vows.

Having my birth father Lyle's sisters present was a reminder of my paternal grandparents, who had instilled in their children strong family values and a commitment to each other to show up and be present in both good and not-so-good times. Lyle, my birth father, showed up when I was fourteen and never stopped being a part of my life.

Grandma Helen, his mom, was the first person he introduced me to as she dug up potatoes in her garden. She impressed me as a parent and grandparent. As a widow, she lived in a tiny apartment but was seldom home. Instead, she traveled between the families of her twelve children, offering support when and wherever needed. She took care of the great-grandchildren and helped with chores and family celebrations. She was loud, opinionated, and an advocate for those in need. My last memory of her was in the summer of 1993. Michael and I attended her funeral in a small country church in Northern Minnesota. During the service, my aunt read a note discovered in Grandma's wallet. It read:

Dear Grandma,

Someday, if I'm ever a grandma, I would like to be like you. Even though we did not meet until I was fourteen, you've taught me a lot about caring for family. Thank you for searching for me. I am so grateful for the day I met you and for the times you came to visit me in California.

Happy Mother's Day!

Debra Marie

My aunt finished, looked up, and walked over to my pew and handed me the note. "Mom cherished this; I think she'd like for you to have it back."

At the end of the service, I visited with my aunts while walking to the graveside. In the distance, I heard Michael call out, " Mom, I'm over here."

He was standing next to a dirt pile with a shovel in his hand, grinning and looking proud to be included in the digging of Grandma's grave; a family tradition originally born out of financial necessity.

FACULTY YEAR TWO, 2014

The university's Christian community was a refreshing change from my former secular work environment. I was encouraged to honor the faith traditions of all students and was expected to integrate one Bible verse into each of the courses I taught. Viewing patients as holistic beings with physical, cognitive, emotional, and spiritual health needs and assessing their needs without personal bias is an expectation of all nurses, one I was enthusiastic about with my students. I had no difficulty discussing spirituality and sharing my faith in the classroom.

As a part of my health assessment course, I taught students how to assess patients' spiritual well-being using evidence-based spiritual assessment tools[15, 16, 17] for discerning the effects of spiritual beliefs on health care. During an in-class exercise, students of many faith backgrounds and agnostics paired with a student who shared a different spiritual belief or religion from their own. Each paired group conducted a spiritual assessment of each other using all three assessment tools. A rich discussion followed as students described their apprehension at the onset of the assignment and eventual rise in comfort level at its conclusion. Students of multiple faith traditions reported the exercise was less stressful than expected because their personal beliefs and biases were irrelevant when using a standardized assessment tool.

FAMILY SUPPORTS

The good news of Garrett's acceptance into all five universities he applied to after struggling to bounce back from dropping out of community college was a testament to his resilience. Unfortunately, the good news was overshadowed by an unexpected diagnosis.

The last thing I told Garrett as I headed to LA for a faculty retreat was, "Double vision is nothing to mess around with. This has been going on for too long. I really think you should go to the emergency room. I talked to Dad about it; he said he would take you, okay?"

I checked in with Steve later that evening; he sounded exhausted. "We've been here all night, and they want to do more tests. It sounds like it might be a while before we know what is going on."

"How's Garrett doing?" I asked.

"He is sleeping on a stretcher, waiting for lab results," Steve informed me.

"Hm, I have no idea what kind of medical workup is necessary for double vision. We need to be patient."

The next day, I called Steve during a break. He was with a buddy from work whom he'd called for moral support.

"Deb, it's not good. Garrett's been diagnosed with multiple sclerosis (MS)."

Before I responded to the shocking news, I recalled symptoms he'd had over several years, including three episodes of vertigo, which had been chalked up to a post-viral syndrome, and the time he asked me, "Mom, why is my arm numb?"

Knowing Garrett wasn't one to make up stories, I recalled examining him and not being too concerned since there was no associated weakness or abnormal reflexes. I told him to tell me if it got worse or did not go away by morning. By morning, it was gone and soon forgotten. I wondered if I'd missed an important finding that would have led to an earlier diagnosis.

"How do they know it's MS?" I asked.

"The ophthalmologist said it showed up on the MRI and in the spinal fluid. A neurologist confirmed the diagnosis and ordered IV steroids to bring down the swelling around the optic nerve. He's home now. A nurse is coming to teach him how to give himself daily injections."

As he finished filling me in, I sensed panic, fear, and dread in his voice. "Steve, this isn't the end of the world; it's an illness that can be treated, not a death sentence. We need to be optimistic and be his cheerleader! No more dread, that's not going to help him," I said, trying to reassure myself as much as him.

I left the retreat early; Garrett's diagnosis made it difficult to concentrate. A few colleagues said a prayer with me before I left. Garret's intermittent fleeting numbness, vertigo, and now unrelenting double vision were the result of nerve damage. His body was destroying the outer layer of his nerve cells, blocking transmission of nerve impulses. It had been going on for a while and had been misdiagnosed by me and several other healthcare providers. MS would require lifelong management. Garrett needed to take charge of his care. My role would be background support. I intentionally left the house the day the home health nurse came to teach him how to give himself daily injections. My absence helped us both.

After the diagnosis, I wanted Garrett to reconsider his university options and stay in town, believing it would be less stressful for him as he was taking on a new challenge. Steve disagreed. "Deb, it's his dream and he earned this, and we can't take it away from him," my husband insisted.

Steve was right, I needed to step aside. I'd watched over Garrett for twenty-five years, advocating for individualized education plans, diagnostic workups, and treatment for ADD without closure, feeling like I'd missed something. It was hard for me to see my purpose as something other than a mom and protector. I had to let go. In the end, I accepted their decision and agreed to monthly campus visits in LA.

REFLECTIONS

Just as the body creates a supportive framework for rebuilding and repairing tissue in wounds, trusting relationships and long-standing academic, medical, and legal professional institutions built on a framework of justice and integrity contributed to my healing.

CHAPTER ELEVEN
BRIDGE AND CLOSE GAPS

San Francisco, Winter 2017

During winter break, I flew north to celebrate my son's and his daughter's birthdays. Steve met me there. He had been camping en route. We invited Audrey, the birthday girl, to spend a night with us at the hotel. Before sunrise, she tapped me on the shoulder and whispered, "Nana, can I go swimming now?"

"Of course you can," I said, not wanting to disappoint her.

We escorted her to the outdoor pool. Steam was rising from the blue glow of the water into the crisp pre-dawn air. We were eager to slip into the warmth of the water. We quietly sang songs from her swimming classes and discussed her upcoming birthday party. We made a memory that morning that would fill the gap in time until our next visit, bridging us into the future.

Before returning home, we spent a day with our daughter, Michelle, driving around the North San Francisco Bay, exploring potential places to move to and housing costs. We decided that if we ever moved closer to our kids, it would have to be farther inland, where real estate was more affordable. The long gaps in time between visits and the distance between us and our Northern California family were wearing us down, motivating us to move closer.

Upon my return home, I directed my attention to lesson plans and my dissertation. Dr. Felitti and the subject of the dissertation topics appeared in an email. My last contact with him was an email introducing me to the work of Jane Stevens, publisher of www.aces-connections.com and www.acestoohigh.com. Her websites provided a wealth of information on the growing scientific evidence surrounding the connections between childhood adversity and long-term health.

Felitti's new email was about the work of Dr. Nadine Burke Harris, a researcher of pediatric toxic stress. He copied Dr. Harris on the message and suggested I contact her. Included in his email was a link to her TED talk about child trauma.[8] I clicked on the link and was delighted to see Dr. Felitti's work explained in such a compelling manner. I shared the link with my HAC friends, students, and anyone interested in public health.

At the advice of my qualitative research professor, Dr. Fry Bowers, I abandoned the idea of researching a topic related to ACES and instead chose a topic I had more expertise in, orthopedics. The research process begins by identifying gaps, which are what is unknown about a topic in scientific literature. After reviewing the orthopedic literature, I discovered gaps concerning the rise in hip fracture rates in men and a second topic, arthroscopic surgery outcomes in patients over forty.

After securing support from Professor BM to chair my dissertation committee, I submitted a proposal to collect information about hip arthroscopy outcomes in partnership with a surgeon. This was a time-consuming and laborious process. I had to abandon the study before it was launched when the surgeon decided to move out of state.

BM challenged me with an observation she made during her advanced quantitative research methods course: "You seem to work alone, not as a team member. Why would I want to chair your committee if you are not comfortable working with a team?"

She was blunt, it stung, and her observation was correct. My original cohort members were not in her class with me, as I advanced ahead of them as a DNP to PhD Bridge student. I was alone and I was miserable and extremely stressed in her class, which was one of the most difficult I had ever experienced. I admired her, and I felt intimidated around her. She eventually agreed to be my chair. However, I had to abandon the study before it was launched, when the surgeon with the hip surgery data decided to work with a medical student instead of me.

A second faculty member agreed to chair my committee in researching hip fracture rates in males, a new gap in the literature since female hip fracture rates had declined following the national implementation of osteoporosis prevention strategies. However, I had difficulty finding research participants, which delayed the process, and I delayed turning in the necessary paperwork confirming my committee membership. I had to start over again when my chair went on sabbatical leave. A three-unit seminar class was required every semester until graduation to guide students in completing the dissertation. I wasted two semesters getting nowhere. I was disappointed with myself and frustrated at having to begin the process again, searching for gaps in the scientific literature and a new research topic.

Overwhelmed by the rising pressure to finish and frustration in my search for a research topic, I began to doubt I'd ever finish the program. I shared my doubts with Steve and my boss, Gayle. Steve said, "It's up to you. Do what you need to do, I'll support you either way."

I wondered if he was a bit relieved. Gayle made the following recommendation: "Debbie, please take your time, pray about it, and hold off on a final decision for a few weeks. I will keep you in my prayers. You have made a huge investment in the program. Take your time before rushing into a decision."

Like Kay, who talked me out of divorce after my first year of marriage, I appreciated Gayle's sound advice. Having a trusted colleague during times of distress temporarily filled the gap of uncertainty and doubt I was feeling. It calmed me as I struggled to clarify my personal and research goals. Taking Gayles's advice renewed my optimism.

The following week, I asked my newest seminar faculty about doing nursing research unrelated to patient outcomes. She assured me that dissertations were not limited to patient outcome studies, dispelling a myth I had heard early in the program. My mind went in a new direction as I assessed the gaps in the literature about orthopedic NP roles. I scheduled a meeting with the director of the PhD program. In the meeting, I realized why I had delayed submitting paperwork and identifying a team of committee members. My need for control held me back from trusting a committee I did not know or have control of. My trust issues resurfaced after the letdown of being replaced by a physician in the hip arthroscopy study. After hearing the PhD chair's suggestions, I gratefully accepted her committee recommendations.

Dr. Georges agreed to be my new chair and guided me in completing a research proposal about subspecialty nurse practitioner roles, a contemporary phenomenon not yet described in scientific literature. The research proposal received approval in March. One member of my committee told me about a conversation she had with an orthopedic surgeon about my proposal. It affirmed my reasons for choosing the topic and sparked enthusiasm to complete the Institutional Review Board (IRB) application. My IRB, crucial for safeguarding research participants and ensuring adherence to regulatory compliance and ethical standards, was approved in May. In June, I began interviewing research participants.

STRENGTH FINDERS

Taking the StrengthsFinder Assessment[18], currently called Clifton's Strengths Assessment, was required by my employer to identify natural talents and strengths. Activator, Connector, Learner, and Context, my dominant strengths, were posted on my office door to remind me and my team where my talents lie. Focusing on my strengths rather than weaknesses boosted my confidence and motivation in the classroom and in the PhD program. However, by the summer of 2017, my ability to multitask was dwindling.

By the fourth year of the PhD program and my fifth consecutive year teaching without a break, I was feeling drained and depleted. The words of my seminar professor, Dr. Mayo, stopped me in my tracks.

"You have already gotten through the hardest part, passing your PhD courses. Finishing the dissertation is the easy part. You already know everything you needed to know for completing the dissertation."

I realized she was right, provided I had the time and energy to complete it. My workload had expanded to teaching the mental health of the older adult with chronic disease (MHOACD) class every semester. The content was heavy. We covered topics like addiction, depression, coping with frailty and disabilities, dementia, caregiver support, burnout, hospice and palliative care decisions, and dying. Many of my students had little lived experience of these complex topics. I invested time recruiting guest speakers to share their perspectives on family caregiver support, patients managing chronic illnesses, and end-of-life experiences. The time and energy needed to teach this course competed with what I needed to complete the dissertation, and more time and energy were needed.

I was granted an unpaid leave of absence for the fall semester to complete my dissertation. I could hardly wait for the end of the summer semester and relief from rising intellectual and emotional demands associated with Mom's hospitalization, Jane's cancer, and my stressful visits to Garrett in LA. And I missed Steve. Being semi-retired, he was enjoying long camping trips in the Sierra Mountains. The dissertation distracted me from missing him and sweet Beau, our new rescue dog, but not enough to ward off evenings of loneliness. Without Beau to cuddle for comfort, I reached instead for popcorn, ice cream, and Netflix. My old bingeing habits resurfaced, triggering memories of shame and self-disgust over my lack of self-control. I needed to find healthier evening distractions, as my weight was creeping up and I was not getting enough sleep.

Teaching MHOACD provided insights into how to be supportive of Jane as she coped with terminal cancer. She was older than my mom, but was like a sister and a mentor to me. We shared family celebrations and holidays, and bonded over being adult children of alcoholics with unhealthy codependent behaviors. After each of her counseling sessions, she shared her insights on overcoming unhealthy codependent behaviors. She was a spiritual advisor in my faith journey and emotional healing. Consequently, being honest and vulnerable with each other came easily. As I shared my pain and frustrations about my mom's drinking, she reminded me about the Alcoholics Anonymous twelve-step program and the message in the Serenity Prayer: to accept what I had no control over and change what I did have control of: myself.

Jane had never married or had children. Support in later years came from her pastor, congregation, and friends from HAC. After retirement, she helped coordinate the annual HAC December Soup Supper gathering for past and present employees. This launched year-round gatherings of lunches, happy hours, and encouraging each other through life celebrations and setbacks, including Jane's recurring cancer.

Summer 2017

I stayed busy teaching my last semester of classes, visiting students in the clinic, and training my replacement for the simulation lab. During one of my last MHOACD classes, I shared a personal story about stigma surrounding mental health care before introducing my guest speaker.

"Before Carol speaks, I would like to give you a little background about myself and our relationship. Despite my nursing education, I subconsciously believed asking for help in overcoming mental health challenges was a sign of weakness until I met Carol. She directed my first medical mission trip to Guatemala. Her skills in organizing and coordinating teams of volunteers to provide services across Guatemala impressed me. During the last weekend in the country, Carol traveled with me to see the Mayan ruins in Tikal. Having her with me, as my interpreter and friend, was comforting. I trusted her completely.

After unpacking our bags in the palm thatched hut we shared, I noticed a prescription bottle on the bathroom sink. I was surprised to learn Carol was on antidepressants, and she felt no need to hide it. She didn't fit my stereotype of someone with depression. Had I known, I may not have volunteered for the mission with her as my leader. I would have unfairly judged her abilities. I learned a valuable lesson that summer about the harm of judging people with mental health challenges. Years later, Carol's friendship and emotional support helped **me** overcome my challenges with depression and anxiety. She is one of my life heroes, and she has agreed to share her patient perspective on treating Depression."

Minnesota Family Wedding

I took a break from working on the dissertation and teaching over the week of July Fourth to attend my uncle Ed's son's wedding with my mom. My seventy-five-year-old mother arranged to take the day off from her part-time job cleaning hotel rooms. The job supplemented her social security income and distracted her from loneliness, especially after my nephew Grant started preschool and she was no longer needed for childcare. During that week, Mom was my first and only priority.

I enjoyed watching Mom get ready for the wedding. She looked just as beautiful to me that day as when I watched her get ready for work as a child. Her slim body, draped in a stylish skirt and caftan, disguised her age. She wore the same short auburn hair, painted on eyebrows, and orange lipstick. The only thing different was her shortened frame and unsteady gait. Mom was not a high-maintenance person; it took little to make her happy. She wasn't a complainer, even though life had gotten more difficult for her. We returned from the wedding in time to watch fireworks from her kitchen window and chat over a glass of wine before bed. The wine let her guard down a bit as she shared with me who her favorite child was, and it wasn't me! It was Paul, my disabled brother. She felt bad after she said it. "Oh, Debra, that wasn't very nice of me, I'm sorry."

"Don't worry, Mom, I understand. I have three kids, and each one is different. It's okay," I assured her.

In my heart, I knew why Paul was her favorite. Mom was a caretaker, and she preferred simplicity. I was complicated, and I didn't need caretaking. We quickly changed subjects, and she talked about the good times with Grandpa Burt and how he helped rebuild her confidence in driving again. I slept well that night, thankful to be with Mom.

Sabbatical

When I returned from Minnesota, Steve and I took a trip to Northern California while I waited for written transcripts of my last two interview recordings. The drive provided ample time for long-overdue conversations. We discussed his semi-retired lifestyle, my dissertation progress, and our desire to relocate to the north.

Steve said, "I knew you couldn't quit, but if you had really wanted to, I would have been okay with it."

"You are right, I couldn't quit. I'm not a quitter, and it's not my way. I am glad I didn't give up," I replied. "I'm getting closer, really! I'll be done by the end of the year when my leave of absence ends."

"About that," Steve said. "When I was camping, I drove to a few places I'd like to show you while we're up north. One is near a university where maybe you could teach, about an hour or so from the kids."

"Yeah, that would be nice. I hate being so far away from them. Seeing everyone twice a year is not enough. We are growing further and further apart and becoming strangers to each other," I lamented.

The words on the tapestry I gave Mom after Don's death tugged on my heart while visiting Michael and Michelle in Northern California.

"To everything there is a season, and a time to every purpose under the heavens."

I had a painful truth to face; it was time to leave Southern California and my teaching position and move closer to my children and grandchildren.

We put an offer on a two-bedroom house that needed a minor renovation near the University of California, Davis. The following week, our house was for sale. We downsized again and packed our belongings into an 8x8x16-foot pod headed for Davis in time for Steve to unload and begin renovations. I stayed behind to close escrow and complete the dissertation. When the house sold, I moved into Jane's guest room.

Jane's hospitality spared me significant financial expenses and provided a welcoming and comforting home during my transition. A few weeks into my stay with her, I realized she hadn't mentioned her deceased mother since I arrived. As an adult child of an alcoholic, I'd sympathized with her and grown accustomed to her complaints.

"Jane, I gotta ask you something," I began.

"Yay... what?"

"I noticed you haven't complained about your mom once since I've been here. How come?"

"Well, a gal from church said, "If you're such a believer in God, why don't you stop complaining, give your painful past to God, and ask for healing?'" she explained. "I realized she had a good point, so I did, and it felt good. I haven't thought about it since."

"Wow! I'm glad she said something to you. You seem more at peace," I observed.

Jane's years of codependency therapy had taught her to keep healthy boundaries. "Deb, I'm offering ya a place to stay, but you're on your own for meals."

Occasionally, I stopped on my way home from campus and picked up her favorite coffee-flavored ice cream to share in the evenings when we watched Netflix together. When she grew tired of watching *Criminal Minds*, she'd say, "That's it, I'm done."

On occasion, I wanted to keep watching, but Jane was tired, so I went to bed. She saved me from binge-watching, sleep deprivation, and loneliness.

On weekends, I helped with chores, and we visited. I was honored to share an intimate and sacred part of her life journey and end-of-life decisions. She shared her beliefs about life after death, her joys, regrets, and the decision to stop cancer treatments and only treat her symptoms. I accompanied her to a palliative care consultation, where she completed an advanced directive articulating her preferences for managing her care if she were unable to speak for herself. I also supported her when she entered hospice care, accepting only comfort care when she discontinued treatments to manage her symptoms. Our conversations prepared me for tough future decisions regarding my mom. Jane and Mom both lived an additional four years, passing during the pandemic within a month of each other.

FINISHING THE PhD

During my quest to complete the PhD, I listened to the advice of several colleagues, including Diana, and marveled at the hardships they faced in completing their own. Diana moved into her office with a sleeping cot and refrigerator to stay focused and avoid wasting time in traffic. Her story inspired me. Grateful for Jane's twin bed, refrigerator space, and exercise room, I kept a strict work schedule. After sharing morning coffee with Jane, I worked out for an hour and left by nine, commuting twenty miles to my office on campus, and returned by 7:00 p.m. I stored food in the breakroom, usually salads for lunch and frozen meals for dinner. Midway through the day, I walked along a nearby river for exercise and sunshine, which eased the tension from hours of leaning over my laptop.

In September, I analyzed and coded each structured interview transcript and my accompanying notes. Questions derived from theories about nurse practitioners and the evolution of subspecies guided my transcript analysis. Each new idea or theme discovered in a transcript was further researched in the literature to ensure that it had not previously been reported.

By October, I noticed consistent themes across all transcripts and looked for what connected them. When connections were not apparent, I dug deeper. I examined the similarities and differences between each transcript that might answer the questions of how and why orthopedic nurse practitioners were used in health care. Once I reached saturation, when information was no longer being discovered in the interviews and literature, I stopped interviewing. I confirmed my findings through a process called triangulation. By the end of the month, I recorded my interpretation of the findings and their significance to nursing and healthcare. I had indeed created new knowledge based on prior knowledge and filled a gap with answers to my research questions.

DISSERTATION—FINAL STRETCH

I sent a copy of my dissertation to my chair for approval to defend it. In early November, while I waited for the dean's review and approval, I visited family and friends in Hawaii. After a birthday gathering for Michelle in Kauai, I left for Oahu, where I stayed with faculty friends. They treated me like a queen, from my airport greeting with a heavenly scented plumeria lei to my morning lattes. The sunrise and sunset walks on Lanikai Beach were exquisite! The sound of waves washed ashore and through me, filling me with peace. It was a joy to experience the hospitality of these ladies who had encouraged me on my PhD journey.

I left the island happy and confident, ready to defend my dissertation findings. Four years of anguish, uncertainty, and the most interesting chapter of my academic journey culminated in the acceptance of my thirty-minute dissertation presentation. The entire experience filled me with a deep sense of admiration, respect, and gratitude for all who have persevered in advancing science, especially my nurse colleagues. Aside from parenting, my brain has never worked so hard.

Dissertation Links to Healing

An unintended outcome of my dissertation journey was discovering links between my research results and conditions that promote sustainable health and healing. I have summarized my research findings below. My digital dissertation is available online[19]

> The orthopedic role is contingent on maturity . . . a necessity for long-term sustainability, the role requires trusting professional relationships . . . and the role is at risk if it continues to emerge away from its core, the nursing model. And lastly, specific environmental conditions contribute to the successful use of ONPs.

Sustainable healing is also contingent on reaching maturation, the final stage of wound healing. Without trusting relationships, personal or professional, there is no foundation for the hope that motivates us towards our healing goals or purpose. Individual healing and sustainable roles are compromised or placed at risk when they deviate from their core or true self. For individuals, that can be one's true self or purpose, and for ONPs, it's the nursing role. Knowing ourselves intimately, what is at our core, brings meaning and purpose into our existence, both individually and professionally.

Lastly, the environment and a mindset of collaboration are necessary for individual healing and the collective well-being of a community. The specialization of nurse practitioners in orthopedics was a response to the scarcity of orthopedic care providers. Collaboration and sharing the gifts of orthopedic physicians and nursing knowledge, skills, energy, and time ensured the orthopedic patient care needs were met and built resilience in the orthopedic healthcare system. Continued successful ONP specialization and healing communities are contingent on building trusting relationships and the sharing of each other's gifts freely, without hoarding or exploiting, to ensure no one in the community has unmet needs. Trust building begins with trusting our values and mission and extends to relationships with others, like physicians, ancillary colleagues, and patients.

Davis, California

Christmas 2017

Living closer to our children increased our opportunities for more personal engagement. Over the holiday weekend, the subject of the ACE study came up in conversation.

"If Felitti's study is correct, my score of nine out of ten ACEs indicates I have an extremely high likelihood of developing chronic illnesses, likely the result of an addiction to a self-soothing behavior."

Not seeing myself as having any addictions, I suggested there could be a mitigating factor, something that builds resilience against addiction. Then my daughter spoke up, ready to correct me.

"Okay, Mom, I think you're kidding yourself if you think you have no addictions."

"What do you mean? Did I tell you about my bulimia when I was younger?"

"No, no, you didn't, that's not what I mean, you're addicted to work! You never stop."

"You think so? I think I'm just a very curious person who loves to learn. You might be right, though." Squirming a bit and feeling under the microscope, I changed subjects. "Does anyone want to go for a walk and burn off some calories? Or we could play games, we've got Risk or Caton."

The truth is that my experiences of multiple childhood adversities, described in Felitti's study, had already taken a toll on me. According to the ACE study[7], a person with a score of 6/10 ACEs has an increased risk for high-risk behaviors contributing toward unplanned pregnancies and STDs, and a 5,000-fold increased risk of attempting suicide! I had not escaped the effects of childhood adversity. I was a ticking time bomb with a 15 percent greater chance of perishing from one of the top ten leading causes of death. According to the study, I have a four times higher risk for chronic depression compared to those with a score of zero. Dr. Felitti's study has been a gift to me, heightening my awareness of the need to be proactive in my healthcare and disease prevention behaviors.

STAGE THREE REFLECTIONS: ACTIONS

Four key events occurred that helped me transition from my orthopedic career to my new role as a nursing professor. The first two were a change in my mindset and self-awareness. This did not happen without discomfort and painful truths. I had to face my fears and insecurities and discover the source of inner strength to overcome them. Through this process, I drew on my past accomplishments and adopted a mindset of opportunity and optimism. The change was made possible by embracing support systems and remaining focused on the present.

Just as supportive cellular structures aid in wound healing, supportive relationships with friends, professional role models, colleagues, and professional services helped me redefine my purpose and heal. My vision of becoming something different was a testament to my hope for a better future and my faith in a higher power that would fulfill my new purpose. This alone was enough reason for me to share my story, to encourage others in both their faith and healing journeys.

As tissue fills the gap across the wound edges, the temporary abundance of blood vessels gradually decreases, as they are no longer necessary. Similarly, as I moved into the maturation stage, I learned to shed the accumulation of that which no longer served my needs. I have begun the process of letting go and defining myself not by what I have lost but by what remains.

As for my addictions, my daughter was correct. After a lifetime of stress, I was addicted to the rush of stress hormones, and I created diversions to both distract me and to maintain the stress hormone high. My need to keep busy served as a distraction from my deep-seated feelings of abandonment and self-doubt. Like escaping the harms of altitude sickness in Guatemala, I had to descend, lower and deeper, letting go of false security, such as job titles and possessions, and inhale the source of all healing: my higher power.

In summary, the third stage of emotional and spiritual healing requires adjusting our behaviors or **actions** that align with our purpose, values, and beliefs. This is accomplished by letting go of harmful beliefs and behaviors and adopting new ones that foster a positive sense of self-worth and healthy relationships.

PART FOUR

TRANSFORMING

MATURATION

In the final and longest stage of wound healing, the wound strengthens and matures to optimize tissue function. This occurs if bleeding has stopped, invaders have been eliminated, adequate defenses are present, and damaged and missing tissue have been rebuilt. During this stage, tissue structures reorganize to increase strength and flexibility in the remaining scar tissue, completing the healing process with improved tissue function.

CHAPTER TWELVE

REORGANIZING

2018-2023

I was without direction or a clear purpose when I moved to Northern California. Everything was in transition: my home, family dynamics, neighborhood, health care, and social and professional relationships. I missed the morning sunrise devotions from my old dining room, as well as familiar faces and places, and the distractions of work and business. My thoughts, feelings, goals, and overall purposes seemed uncertain. It was the first time in my life that I was living without a three-year plan, and I was eager for direction. I sought guidance in a heartfelt talk with the Creator of the Universe, my higher power. Direction came with a simple message: "Read the words and reflect daily on messages you receive from The Lord's Prayer."

This was not what I expected. However, I embraced it and journaled daily on whatever came to mind as I reflected on the words from Matthew 6:9-13.[20] The pages filled up quickly. Six years later, I have two full notebooks of insights and revelations that have challenged my thoughts and beliefs and provided guidance.

The day I met Mayor Davis at the farmer's market was when my days got brighter. He was hosting a sign-up table for volunteers. I introduced myself as a retired nurse and newcomer to the area and asked him for volunteer recommendations. I was surprised and delighted with his line of questioning and eventual recommendation to get involved with Resilient Yolo (RY), an affiliation of the ACEs Connection online community and later PACES Connection. He also connected me by email with members in the RY community. Their goal of educating individuals and organizations on the effects of childhood adversity and the means of building resilience attracted me.

I immersed myself in RY activities. Monthly meetings exposed me to community experts in resilience building through trauma-informed practices. This group practiced what they preached. Self-care and resilience-building practices were included in their meetings and lifestyles. The five principles of Trauma-Informed Practice—safety, trustworthiness, choice, collaboration, and empowerment—guided their meetings and entire agenda. Meetings began with reflections on meditative readings or relaxation practices, such as guided imagery or deep breathing exercises. They offered healthy snacks, and discussions were inclusive and respectful. They inspired me to incorporate more self-care and resilience practices into my own personal life.

Attending Resilient Yolo[21] events and learning about the principles of trauma-informed practices clarified the effects of trauma in my life and inspired me to implement and share the principles with others.

In 2019, I facilitated a six-week course at a community church about ACES and trauma-informed practices, exploring their connections with sacred scriptures. I used the TED Talk by Dr. B. Harris[8] and material found on the ACES Connection website. One of the class participants, a physician, shared her frustration: "I'm really mad I was never taught this material in medical school. I would have approached patient care very differently if I had. This class has changed my approach to patient care."

Another comment in the class evaluation suggested I advertise more and offer larger classes, as the material was highly informative and essential. I also had one participant drop out of the class because it triggered uncomfortable thoughts, which reminded me of a discussion with Dr. Felitti, in which he shared one of the conditions required by the IRB reviewing the ACE Study[7] proposal. Participants in the study were required to be provided with an emergency hotline phone number to call if they experienced psychological distress while completing the survey. He said no one ever called the number. However, individuals did send him written thank-you notes for asking the questions that validated their adverse childhood experiences. He also shared a possible unintended consequence of the study: the number of primary care appointments dropped significantly in the year following the survey.

Community Engagement

Daily reflections drew me to three activities: volunteering with the League of Women Voters, researching my ancestral roots, and investigating local teaching options. After completing an online, lengthy credentialing process, I was disappointed to learn the U C Davis School of Nursing was in Sacramento, a forty-five-minute commute from my home. Recalling Michelle's comments about me being addicted to work, I agreed to be a guest lecturer on orthopedic topics and work in the simulation lab only when needed, as an unpaid volunteer faculty member. I was giving permitting myself to stop working.

Joining the League of Women Voters turned into a rewarding and satisfying volunteer position on the Health Committee. I participated in creating informative and well-received community forums surrounding the topics of healthcare costs and access. We transitioned to an online format during the pandemic, which enabled us to recruit qualified speakers and invite participants from a broader audience beyond our local community. Collaborating with the highly committed and well-informed committee members inspired and nurtured me socially, emotionally, and intellectually. More importantly, the opportunity to contribute to meaningful activities renewed my sense of purpose.

Our Davis real estate agent gave me a one-year membership to the University Farm Circle (UFC), a philanthropic organization that helps local university students and provides an immense network of social activities for its members. Her gift was instrumental in enhancing my joy in discovering a social life in Davis. Through UFC, I joined a garden club, a dinner club, a wine tasting group, and a book club. The book club was the hardest to let go of when we moved in 2019. I'll touch on that change later. The ladies came from all backgrounds and offered new and engaging perspectives on our readings. The camaraderie and friendship proved more important than the books we read.

To explore my ancestral roots, my mom and I took a road trip through Wisconsin, where Grandpa Frank's family had settled after immigrating from Germany in the mid-1800s. We visited historical societies, libraries, and cemeteries, and discovered that when grandpa's grandfather was ten years old, he experienced the death of his father. I wondered if this childhood adversity, compounded with other events, contributed to five generations of alcoholism in my family. Our days ended with dinner and conversation in a cozy Italian restaurant near our hotel.

"It's nice to see you enjoying yourself, eating out, and staying in a hotel rather than cleaning it, right, Ma?"

"It sure is," she said with a cute smile, followed by, "We'll have to be sure we leave her a nice tip. I appreciate tips."

The following morning, while loading the rental car, I stopped Mom as she dragged her suitcase across the parking lot. "Leave that for me, Mom. I'll get it."

In her typical headstrong fashion, she said, "No, you don't have to, I can do it."

Why does she insist on doing it herself? I wondered. *She can barely walk.*

Is it the years of waiting on my dad and him never lifting a finger to help?
I figured she would have gotten past her stubbornness by now, after
living with Grandpa Burt, who always helped her, but I was wrong.

"MOM! For Pete's sake, I'm your daughter, it's the least I can do!"
I yelled across the lot. "Why do you insist on depriving me of the joy
of helping my mother? You would help your mother, wouldn't you?
Really, Mom, think about it."

She started to smile and let go of her suitcase, reaching to cover
her face as though she was embarrassed, and laughed at herself. " Of
course, you're right, I don't know why. Thank you, Debra," she said as
she stepped aside so I could lift her bag into the trunk.

Native American Ancestors

After leaving Mom's house in Duluth, I drove alone, south to Wabasha,
Minnesota, to discover my Native American heritage dating back to
the French fur traders in the 1600s. The town was named after Chief
Wabasha, an ancestor on my father's side. Eager to learn about my
family ties to the community, I headed to the library, where I found
a book about the history of Wabasha, MN, which depicted life from
the mid-1700s to the mid-1800s.[22] I wept reading about the slaughter
of Native women and children and the forced evacuation of Native
Americans from their home state. I left the library sad and disturbed
at the omission of this information from my history lessons growing
up. I wandered around town until I came across streets named after
my Native American ancestors, Agustin and Angelique La Roque, and
land that another ancestor donated for a church cemetery. My mood
improved as I walked through the cemetery and discovered the burial
site of my Native American great-great-grandmother, Philomena. I felt
a spiritual connection and yearned to learn more about my ancestors.

Learning of the intergenerational trauma within my Minnesota
family and Native American ancestors stirred up compassion and new

insights regarding unhealthy behaviors in myself and other family members. I wondered if and how elevated levels of stress hormones associated with historical trauma may have altered my or my children's genetic makeup and behavioral responses.

Discovering the concept of being re-traumatized and the benefits of being trauma-informed, sensitive to the painful experiences of others and myself, was the highlight of my life in Davis. Through these lessons or insights, I developed a newfound sense of self-compassion, a necessary part of my own healing. I forgave myself for not returning to work in the classroom, reminding myself that my value was not dependent on my accomplishments or paycheck. I also promised myself that I would seek more joy in life and make more of an effort to understand others through the lens of being trauma-informed.

When I was in Davis, I joined a city-wide book club that was reading *The Book of Joy*.[23] Lessons from the book inspired me to live life with less suffering, stress, and sadness, despite the current challenges within my family. I also decided to book a river cruise with Steve in 2019 after Mom's eightieth birthday.

2019: CELEBRATION

After much indecision, Mom finally decided to sell her house and move into the senior living apartment where her friend lived. In March, I helped her fill out and submit the paperwork online for subsidized housing in a building overlooking Lake Superior. The average wait time to occupancy was nine months. We anticipated a December move-in date.

In May, our family traveled to celebrate Mom's eightieth birthday. We hosted a party at Mom's former place of employment, *The Pickwick*. Mom's health had declined significantly. No longer able to walk without aid, she had quit her job. She shuffled her feet in oversized shoes to accommodate the swelling in her feet and used a walker to get around.

I was surprised to learn she was still driving, given that we had to lift her into and out of our rental car. While we were there, Mom accepted an offer on her house with a July closing date.

I returned in July to help put my mom's furniture in storage and move her temporarily into my brother Vincent's house. Disconnecting insurance, phone, cable, and utilities was a complicated process, as her bills were on automatic payment and she no longer used a computer and couldn't recall her passwords. Also, mobility difficulties prevented her from settling accounts in person. I wondered how she and other people who were frail, elderly, and computer illiterate would manage without an advocate. I see an entire industry forming to address the needs of this population.

We outgrew our Davis home when Garrett moved back home. We moved to a larger place ten miles away in Winters, California, a town with a population of only 7,000. Complications from multiple sclerosis affected his academic progress and eventual decision to quit school. Crossing county lines adversely affected his access and eligibility for healthcare after leaving college, which was a significant source of stress for both of us. By fall, we were all settled in with ample room for Garrett and visits from Michael's family.

Anxious to find a meaningful place in our new community, Steve and I volunteered to deliver Meals on Wheels to homebound seniors, and I volunteered on the new Senior Winter Commission on Aging as an advisor to the city council. We stopped delivering when COVID hit, but I stayed on the commission, acclimating to online meetings. As chair of the commission, I represented the city on the county senior commissions during the pandemic, advising on ways to keep seniors safe in their homes and community living environments. Serving as a representative on the city and county commissions alongside outstanding and caring community leaders was an informative, enriching, and enjoyable experience.

We held an open house on New Year's Day 2020 for the first

fourteen families who had moved into the new housing development on the outskirts of town. Our guests shared their moving experiences and exchanged contact information with one another. As weeks passed, we exchanged pleasantries next to mailboxes and invited neighbors over for meals and to watch football games. I was grateful for our early introductions and the chance to connect names with faces and houses in our growing community. These connections helped sustain our relationships as neighbors during the pandemic.

Mom's lake-view apartment was ready in February 2020. I helped update her financial records to ensure she remained eligible and arranged for movers to deliver her belongings. I arrived the night before and stayed with Kay. It was nice to have a friendly listening ear and to catch up on each other's lives.

The following morning, I drove Mom to her new apartment and introduced myself to LuLue, the apartment manager, and provided her with my contact information in case of an emergency. Mom had been collecting new things for her apartment for eleven months. I unpacked two new hair dryers, three new curling irons, and duplicate kitchen items, confirming my suspicion that she was becoming forgetful. I stayed for a week to help her get settled. I installed a portable shelving unit in her walk-in pantry, ensuring that all items were within easy reach, as she was no longer able to reach into lower cupboards or top shelves. The last thing we did together was shop for groceries and visit Vince and his son Grant. I was uneasy about leaving Mom. I wished she were in an assisted living home rather than an independent living arrangement. I promised myself I'd return as soon as possible to make the change. As I left her apartment, I said, "Mom, everyone's phone number is on the white board by the phone. Please remember to ask Lynette from the fifth floor for help if you need it, and do not forget to ask Vincent for help."

CHAPTER THIRTEEN

REVISING

The onset of the pandemic coincided with multiple revisions in our routines, relationships, and responsibilities. My attention moved from volunteer work to family caregiving. Mom sustained a head injury that required hospitalization a week after moving into her new apartment. My telephone conversation with her doctor was enlightening for both of us.

"Your mother has mild cognitive impairment," explained Dr. M. "What are you basing that assessment on?" I asked. –

"The Montreal Cognitive Assessment. Her score was 20/30," he replied, and elaborated further about his recent visit with Mom.

" Much of what you are describing about Mom has been normal for my mother her entire life," I said, followed by specifics about her usual behaviors.

"I see," he said with a pause. "I think your mother is on the autism spectrum. I'm so sorry I didn't make the connection earlier. It's only been in recent years that I've been made aware of the diagnosis. In fact, my own sister, in her sixties, was recently diagnosed with being on the autism spectrum. Now that I think about it, I recall your mother has always exhibited signs of being on the autism spectrum, like resistance to being examined, minimal eye contact, minimal displays of emotions, and difficulty discussing her feelings. I recall uncomfortable conversations with her when she's been blunt, to the point, and rude."

"Yes, that's my mother; she's always been like that," I agreed. "Her way of coping with uncomfortable issues has always been to ignore and avoid them or lash out and distract. I'm not surprised at the mild cognitive impairment; I've noticed it and wondered if alcoholism had contributed to it. I believe her impairment is not significant enough to warrant forcing her to move into assisted living, as she can do laundry, cook, and pay her bills. However, I realize this is likely to change over time. If possible, I'd like her to be referred to assisted living when she is discharged from the hospital and to have her driving ability assessed. I think she is a danger to herself and others if she continues to drive her car."

"I will refer her to physical therapy for the driver's assessment exam and the hospital social worker for discharge planning," he stated.

Mom called a cab and left the hospital against medical advice, refusing to transfer to a skilled nursing facility for continued physical therapy to improve her strength and steady her gait. Her doctor arranged for home health services to supervise her medication management, heart failure symptoms, and ability to provide self-care. Three different RNs attempted to gain her trust before I convinced Mom to allow Candy, an RN from the College of Saint Scholastica, to visit her on a weekly basis. From March until September, during the COVID pandemic, Candy checked in with Mom. In May, when her insurance coverage was ready to run out, I convinced her doctor to extend her services for management of weepy wounds in her swollen lower legs. Care was extended until the end of August, when I planned to visit her. Mom was strong-willed and took pride in being self-sufficient, which supported her sense of dignity. I walked a fine line with her, trying to protect her dignity while keeping her safe.

Winters, California, 2019-2021

Moving to a new community resulted in a change in health insurance plans and health care providers for Garrett, Steve, and me. I spent many hours on the phone to find and activate the services. Our monthly health insurance premiums doubled when my California COBRA plan ran out, as the availability of service during COVID declined.

We were unable to see an in-person provider when Steve developed signs of a mini-stroke. I listened to his phone consult with his new physician as Steve said, "I've talked on my feet for years in the court-room, and I never had a loss for words until this week."

His old doctor would have recognized the changes in his speech patterns as I did. The call ended with a recommendation to monitor his symptoms. Thankfully, they did not progress.

On Easter, my plans to deliver Easter baskets to my two grand-daughters in San Francisco were altered to include the delivery of an overnight bag to the emergency room where Michael, their forty-nine-year-old father, was admitted for a heart attack and surgery. Unable to visit with the girls, I waved and called out, "I love you," and left the baskets at the bottom of the staircase as I retrieved Michael's bag for delivery. That evening, while he was in surgery, I developed non-cardiac chest pain. Perhaps it was sympathy pain for Michael.

During our time in Winters, our daughter-in-law was finishing a doctorate in education on weekends while working as a teacher during the week, and Michael was working two jobs. We looked forward to visits from Michael and the girls on weekends when his wife was in class. Aside from the girls, my primary distraction and stress reliever was bingeing on Netflix and Garret's delicious baked goods. To keep busy, he cooked for us while perfecting his culinary skills. Nurse Mel from *Virgin River* and Claire from *Outlander* entertained and distracted me nightly from the national news, the uncertainties surrounding the pandemic, and challenges at home.

DULUTH, MINNESOTA, AUGUST 2020

Six months after moving Mom into the senior apartment, I booked an Airbnb near her new place for five weeks, anxious to check in on her. I had quarantined for two weeks before and wore a mask and face shield on the plane. I planned to work on my memoir in the mornings and spend the afternoons and evenings with Mom. I had not yet started writing, but I had condensed forty years of my diary entries into ten pages of notes regarding key life-changing memories. I reviewed my notes for a general theme, which I decided was healing. Each morning, I pulled out relevant memories associated with the healing theme and assigned them a place in my outline. Mornings were painful, as I relived challenging times in Duluth. I visited the maternity home, now a board and care facility, and walked by my old foster home. Every neighborhood called up memories. Some were good, but most were not.

My afternoon routines included shopping, errands, and eating out with Mom, because she didn't want a messy kitchen. On Tuesdays, I took her to the beauty salon. In the mornings, she cleaned her apartment and read the paper. She was usually watching Fox News when I arrived around noon. Our evenings were special. She shared her life stories, previously unknown to me. These stories helped me get to know her more intimately, especially after we had been living apart for over forty years.

There are three outstanding memories from that visit worth sharing. The first was the conversation following an episode of *60 Minutes* that featured end-of-life issues, like living in assisted living and nursing homes, and an interview with the author of *Being Mortal: Medicine and What Matters in the End* by Atul Gawande[24], a book I had required NP students to read in my MHOACD course. The other two memories are of the day we visited an orphanage and a nearby cemetery, as well as my final in-person conversation with her.

At the end of the program, I asked my mom, "So, Mom, have you given any thought to what'll happen to you when you die?"

"Of course I have," she answered.

"Well, what do you think? What's gonna happen?" I prodded.

"The nuns taught us, you know, with the prayer," she said

"What prayer, Mom?"

She hesitated, trying to recall the prayer. I named a few that I knew of, like the 23 Psalms, and she shook her head, "No, that's not the one the nuns taught."

"Do you remember it? Can you recite it from memory?"

She nodded as she said: "Now I lay me down to sleep; I pray the Lord my soul to keep. If I should die before I wake, I pray the Lord my soul to take. It's just that simple, Debra, there's nothing to worry about."

Her childlike faith and simplicity amazed me and touched me with a sense of calm.

I got a glimpse of Mom's childhood when we visited the orphanage where she lived with her siblings for three years. Our drive along the long and winding county roads was spectacular. Clear blue skies were interrupted by trees crowned with bright yellow, orange, and crimson leaves lining the way to the former orphanage. Perched on a hill within the expansive property was a large four-story red brick building. We spent the next hour walking around the property as she described her chores and pointed out various features, including the interior dining hall, chapel, and the separate dorms for girls and boys.

"Debra, it wasn't bad, it was like a fine finishing school, we even had music lessons," she shared with a grin. "They took good care of us."

She talked about life across the four seasons, skating on the ice-skating rink made by the priest and playing tag near the summer garden by the barn where the boys milked cows, and the fall harvest picked by the girls under the watchful eye of the nuns.

Mom was able to distill her experience at the orphanage into positive ones. I, too, have come to recognize my early life experiences as positive ones. They prepared me to be flexible and adaptable, the necessary attributes of an intensive care and emergency room nurse, and essential elements for working in the ever-changing environment of orthopedics.

REVISED HISTORY

Later that evening, Mom continued sharing stories from her new electric recliner that she ordered by phone from the local hospital supply store. Not only did it recline, but at the push of a button, it aided her in standing and dismounting from it. Mom was now sleeping in the recliner because her heart failure made it difficult to lie flat. Apparently, I could have stayed in her bedroom and not rented a room, but I'm glad I did. I liked the privacy while working on the memoir. Sitting on the nearby sofa, I encouraged Mom to continue.

"Did I ever tell you about Chuck?" she asked. "I dated him when I moved back to Watertown, after leaving you in Colorado with the nuns at the orphanage."

This was the first time my mother had ever mentioned leaving me at an orphanage. However, I had suspected it.

"He was tall and a good-looking guy. We had plans to go to a barn dance. At the last minute, I cancelled our date. Debra, I can't tell you why," she paused. "I don't know why. I just decided not to go. He went anyway, with another girl. On the way to that dance, his car was hit head-on. He and his date were killed. Debra, that was the last possible week for me to get you from the orphanage, before my six months ran out, and you would be adopted. I had a plane ticket to go and get you. Grandpa bought it for me. I was going back to get you. I can't imagine what would have happened to you if I'd gone with Chuck that night."

We both sat in silence as I let this news sink in. With courage, forged by love and faith, she had done the unthinkable. Was it the narrow escape from death that fueled her courage, confirming her purpose as my mother? She was finally able to admit that she had left me in an orphanage. Her guard was down, so I asked more questions.

"Mom, my dad told me he wanted to marry you. And Grandma Betty admitted to meeting his parents. She wasn't impressed, I guess; she said their 'cows were too skinny.' I saw the unsigned marriage license. I know Grandma wouldn't give permission because you were only seventeen. But you could have married my dad three months later without Grandma's permission. You could have married at eighteen, but why didn't you?"

"My parents said no, and I was raised to obey my parents because they knew what was best for me," she explained. "Debra, I'm sorry things were so hard for you. I couldn't leave Don; I couldn't handle you kids by myself. I needed him to be in charge."

"I understand, Mom," I assured her. "Things were different back then. I'm glad you got me. It must have been hard for you." In that moment, I released my past pain, anger, and judgment of my mom. My heart softened with gratitude for her refusal to accept the finality of leaving me in Colorado, and I was grateful for her courage and the love that motivated her to ignore societal expectations, parental authority, and the unyielding stigma of being an unwed mother in the 1950s. She gave me all that she had, herself, in the only way she knew how: out of love.

"It was hard, I didn't even know how to change a diaper," she recalled. "I asked the man sitting by me on the plane if he knew, but he said no. And Grandma didn't want the relatives to know, so I found a nice foster home for you until I had enough money to move to Duluth with you. She was a nurse, and she wanted to adopt you."

I knew the rest of the story. She met my stepdad at Hotel Duluth, where she worked in the coffee shop. He had just gotten off the ore boats, where he was working as a cook. Grandpa Frank watched me while she worked. They married when I was two.

I waited a few weeks before bringing up the subject of finding an assisted living facility. She agreed to visit a few with me. At the conclusion of our site visits, parked outside of her apartment before heading in, I asked Mom if she would be interested in moving into one of the places we visited. Her entire demeanor changed. She crouched down in her seat, bent forward, covered her head with her arms, yelling, "No! Absolutely not! No! I'm not like you, I don't think like you, I never have!" Then her voice changed from a yell to a cry, "I don't want to live in those places, I just want to be left alone!"

Her pain was palpable to me, and I felt terrible for causing it. I wanted her to be safe. Unable to provide her with a safe and caring home, I wanted to ensure she had someone advocating for her. Living with me wasn't an option at the time. She had a fear of flying, and I was afraid of heights and driving over mountains, especially in the winter. Even if I could, I worried about her heart failure, incontinence, and contracting COVID. Truthfully, I was not sure if Steve and I could manage the stress of living with her without sabotaging our relationship. What I was sure of was my inability to continue the conversation or spend the rest of the day with her. I was exhausted and helpless.

"Mom, I'm sorry I upset you. I won't push the issue any further," I assured her. "You have the right to decide where and how you want to live, and I respect that. You have already made a huge change, giving up your home and moving into the apartment. I am going to unload the groceries and call it a day. I need a break. I will be back tomorrow in time to bring you to your hair appointment. I love you."

I cried quietly under the blankets in my rented room. I felt impotent and angry, powerless in convincing Mom to move to a safer environment, and angry about everything, including her stubbornness and the fact that there was no one to help me. Her stubbornness and lack of insight into the situation triggered childhood memories of frustrating conversations about my brother Paul's needs and challenges, and Dad's abuse, especially when Mom drank. The same frustration and pain I felt then returned. I was beginning to see Mom as a person on the autism spectrum who used alcohol to medicate her anxiety. She was like her father; they both were anxious people who avoided their pain with alcohol and avoidance behaviors. For years, I concluded that Mom's behaviors were the result of childhood adversities, including divorce, parental mental health problems, and abandonment at the orphanage. I now believe the combination of ACES, genetics, and the effects of chronic alcoholism all contributed to her unhealthy coping mechanisms and lifestyle. Living under the watchful eye of Don and later Grandpa Burt had been stabilizing factors, and now she had no one. Mom believed a man should be in charge, no matter what. I figured it was a generational expectation of traditional gender roles. Now I realized it was more than that; she needed someone in charge because it provided comfort.

Like the necessary moisture that aids in wound healing, the tears I shed that afternoon were healing; they released tension and cleared my thoughts. I recognized my need for help in getting through my fear and anger. I called a friend with Al-Anon experience, seeking advice and comfort. We had been friends for thirty years since meeting at Garrett's preschool, and I trusted her. She spoke kind words and offered insightful responses to my questions and insecurities in managing my relationship with my mom. Reaching out to her was unforeseen, as it wasn't my usual means of handling pain. I was learning how to be vulnerable with a friend as a way of caring for myself. It felt good.

Before leaving Minnesota, Mom agreed to call me once a day to let me know she was okay, and to just hang up if she did not want to talk. She hated talking on the phone, and this seemed like a reasonable compromise. I was comfortable leaving her on her own to manage medications, since she had been taking them without prompting. I reminded my brother Vincent to check in on her, to help with groceries and opening cartons and cans, stressing how vulnerable she had become.

My younger brother, Paul, was not reliable; he had problems since birth, problems that Mom was finally able to talk about before I left. After years of denial, Mom shared the truth about my cognitively impaired, four-foot-seven brother who suffered from a severe speech impediment and unusual facial features.

"Before Paul turned eighteen, the social workers recommended we appoint a guardian and conservator for him. They tried to warn us; they said he'd have a hard time living on his own once he got out of the group homes. Don didn't believe them. He insisted Paul would be fine. We should have taken their advice, Debra."

Having done my own assessment of Paul, I agreed. To lighten the mood, I said, "At least Lee helped him get on Social Security disability."

She nodded in agreement. I paused, recalling Lee, my deceased sister, wondering if Mom was thinking about her, too.

CHAPTER FOURTEEN
ALTERING FORM AND FUNCTION

October 2020

As I reached for the phone, I recognized Mom's number and hoped I would be able to talk with her, but she wasn't in the mood. "This is just my call, we don't need to talk," she insisted.

"Wait, please don't hang up, Mom! I'd really like to talk with you."

"I need to wash my hair; I can't talk now," she said, and for the first time ever, rather than accept her blunt, rude reply, I interrupted and challenged her.

"Mom, I think it will take you twenty minutes out of your day to wash your hair. I miss talking with you, I care about you, and I want to know how you are getting along. Are you sure you cannot spare five minutes to indulge me?"

"Of course I can, Debra, I don't know what's a matter with me. You're right, my hair can wait," she sheepishly replied.

In an instant, I realized that this was the approach I should have been taking for years. I had been too intimidated to own the adult version of me, and responded like a child, accepting my mom's rude and often inappropriate behaviors without challenging them. I now knew she didn't mean to be rude; she just said and did things without realizing how others interpreted her words and actions. I accepted her rude and often inappropriate responses without understanding the rejection, resentment, and pain it was causing me. In reflecting on our conversation, I recognized my failures to prioritize my self-care when accepting rude and inappropriate behaviors of others. We had a short, pleasant conversation about her friend on the fifth floor and why she wasn't going to the beauty shop. In the tension of our call, I learned to be more direct when communicating with Mom, and not to make assumptions about her.

January 2021, Winters

Four months later, Mom's apartment manager called me with disturbing news.

"Debra, I'm calling to tell you your mom fell and hit her head. Your brother Paul asked me to check on her when she didn't answer her door for him. She was awake and alert but too weak to get up off the kitchen floor. Her head was bleeding, so we called an ambulance. She's on her way to the hospital now."

Mom's admission to the hospital was twofold: one, to evaluate the extent of her head injury, and two, to stabilize her heart. She had stopped taking her heart medications, which had caused twenty pounds of excessive fluid to accumulate in her system, straining her heart. Once stable, she was transferred to the cardiac floor, where her regular doctor assessed her.

Mom's doctor suggested that I become her conservator and guardian, as she was no longer physically or mentally able to participate in managing her care. He also suggested placement in hospice because she had end-stage terminal heart and liver disease and an inoperable brain injury. My copy of my mom's advance directive guided my decisions in her final days.

FEBRUARY 2021

THE END IS NEAR

In early February, via a Zoom meeting, the court granted me guardianship and conservatorship of my mom at the recommendation of her court-appointed attorney and physician. I spoke with Mom the night before she left for hospice. The conversation is still clear in my mind. I was sitting on a swivel chair at my kitchen counter. She was less confused than the day before, and we had a pleasant conversation.

"Debra, I will be back in my apartment before you know it. I just need to get stronger."

As her daughter and a nurse, it was my job to support her by not diminishing her hope, so I refrained from correcting her. I said: "Mom, I just want what is best for you, you know that, right?"

Her final words before the call ended, and as it turned out, the last words she would ever speak to me, were, "I know, you're the perfect daughter."

Weeks later, that conversation played out in my mind. Words matter, especially the last ones you hear. She blessed me with kindness that day, even when I didn't believe I deserved it.

I called the nursing home in the morning to arrange the delivery of flowers to cheer her up. The nursing home personnel who answered said, "I'm so glad you called! We were just looking for your number. Your mother's been here for about an hour. We don't expect her to live beyond the day. If anyone wants to be with her, they should come now. You should call them now."

Shocked, I said, "Are you sure? Her doctor said it could be weeks or months."

"Yes, her legs are blue; she has all the signs," the voice said.

"Can I talk to her?" I asked.

"Yes, call back in a few minutes, and I'll get someone to hold the phone for her," they assured me.

In the next ten minutes, I called my brother Vincent, her brother Ed in Saint Paul, and the priest to administer last rites. Then I called back. The nurse put the phone near Mom's ear.

"Hi, Momma, it's Debbie. Uncle Ed and Vince are coming to see you today."

I heard a faint whisper, "Okay," and then she drifted off.

Three hours later, Ed called me from Mom's bedside.

"Debbie, I'm so sorry to tell you, your mom has died. She knew I was in the room. I had to put on isolation clothes first, and then I got to see her. I held her hand, and then I remembered you telling me the story about a special prayer, so I repeated it to her: Now I lay me down to sleep, I pray the Lord my soul to keep. If I should die before I wake, I pray the Lord my soul to take. Debbie, she tried to mouth the words. When I finished, she took her last breath. She was waiting for me; I am sure of it. I am so glad I was with her. I love my big sister. She was always there for me when I was little. This was special. Thank you for calling me."

As I hung up from the call, I felt the weight and chaos of the past week lift; it was over, although sooner than expected. I was angry and relieved at the same time. Angry that Mom died four hours after transferring her on the coldest day of the year. I let my frustration be known to the hospital discharge planner, and in the end, accepted their explanation that they had no idea she was so close to dying. Mom was more in control than I will ever know. She hated being touched and being dependent on others, and she didn't like nursing homes. She ended life on her terms.

MARCH 3, 2021

DULUTH, MINNESOTA

Arriving in Duluth felt surreal; the sky was grey with snow flurries, and the air was colder than I expected. I exited the taxi in front of the high-rise apartment and reached for my rolling suitcase. The chilly air awakened my senses and reminded me that I had forgotten my gloves. My mission was clear, but emotionally overwhelming. I needed to empty Mom's apartment. It had been less than a month since her death, and now I would close this chapter of her and my life in just four days.

The apartment was quiet and lifeless, except for the hissing of the heater. Everything was as I remembered, except the wooden kitchen table was in the living room. According to the apartment manager, Mom fell while reaching into the refrigerator and slid under the table. She was awake but confused when the paramedics arrived. I glanced at the electric recliner, recalling Mom comfortably drifting off to sleep under her favorite crocheted blanket as I left for the airport five months earlier. I thought I would see her again. The stark finality of her absence settled on me like that morning's dusting of snow. It would melt, and I would somehow move on, truly orphaned.

The next few days blurred into a frenzy of packing boxes, coordinating donations, and hauling out furniture. The physical labor was exhausting, and the emotional weight of the experience would have drained me if not for family and friends who came by to help and visit. They kept me company while I waited for customers generated from Facebook Marketplace to show up one at a time to claim their new possessions. The pandemic had limited options for unloading household goods. I took photos of everything with my cell phone and posted them on Facebook and online rummage sales sites. I invited my aunt and uncle over to see if there was anything they wanted to have to remember Mom by. I recalled how Mom had appreciated their help shoveling her driveway when she still had the house. They invited my cousins to join us. Their presence during my time of grief was comforting. The same was true of my childhood friends who arrived with packing boxes.

Daily, I delivered well-received boxes of clothes and knick-knacks to the community room, and each day they disappeared into someone's apartment. Mom would have been pleased. I set aside a suitcase full of photos to go home with me, along with my mom's bedside chest, a wedding gift from Grandpa Burt to her, and then finished vacuuming.

Finding her burial plans triggered a memory of the day we visited the cemetery on the way to the orphanage. She wanted to ensure her recently purchased grave marker had been engraved, and for me to see the one she had bought for Paul. She insisted that Paul not be buried in an unmarked grave when he died. That was when she told me her obituary and funeral plans were in her top drawer. I needed to put those thoughts aside, but it was hard to stay focused. I was tired and hungry, and I needed a break.

I called Carmen to join me for dinner. I looked forward to seeing her and wondered if she'd have suggestions for what to do with Mom's remaining few items. We had been friends since high school, where we met in a support group for teen moms. Five members of the group remained friends for over fifty years. It was in 2010 when we had our first reunion in Las Vegas, and we met again in Minnesota in 2023. Our shared experiences connected us, offering a sense of camaraderie with one another as resilient mothers and now as grandparents.

I ran down nine flights of stairs to meet Carmen and entered the lobby as a lady in her mid-sixties approached wearing an unusual mask. *Oh my God, that is the funniest mask I've ever seen,* I thought as she approached me. Her mask bore a fat set of bright red lips with a large toothy grin, like what you would see on a clown's face. The next thing

I heard was her boisterous belly laugh and the comment, "I came to cheer you up," and that she did.

Listening to my body and honoring its needs was gradually becoming second nature, and during this difficult week, it paid off. Seeing Carmen eased my sadness and loneliness during a painful experience. That night was my last night in Mom's bed. I slept well.

My last task was to clean Mom's refrigerator. It contained half a bottle of vodka, orange juice, and condiments. The freezer contained a half loaf of bread and something wrapped in plastic that looked like meatloaf. Mmm, my favorite. I opened the microwave, discarded an old Lean Cuisine dinner from who knows when, and defrosted the bread and meatloaf. The odor triggered my taste buds. "Thanks, Mom," I said aloud as though she were in the room.

It was a perfect way to end this day, lunch with Mom, comforted by the comfort food of my youth. Realizing that her early dementia had not prevented her from cooking for herself. I said a prayer, thanking God for the moment of comfort. Next, I turned in her keys and headed to the hotel next door, where my uncle Ed and his family were waiting to pack up the last of Mom's belongings and then take me to the airport.

May 20, 2021

Cemetery

We gathered at the graveside to celebrate Mom's life on what would have been her eighty-second birthday. An indoor memorial seemed impractical given the potential risks to her elderly friends of contracting the COVID-19 virus. About ten of us, including waitresses, neighbors, and family, assembled under a canopy. All who were present participated in meaningful ways, and no one seemed to notice that the minister, who was fearful of driving in the rain, had cancelled. Guests shoveled dirt into the hole and on top of Mom's container of ashes as they shared their memories of Mom. Their comments anointed me with new perspectives about her.

"Marie never let anyone get her down, not even when the boss unfairly yelled at her. She'd say, 'Okay, girls, we've got work to do; we're not going to let him ruin our night.'"

"She was strong, a hard worker, and she never complained."

"She accepted people and didn't try to change them."

"I never heard her say a bad word about anyone."

This one I knew to be true, as Mom often said, "If you can't say anything nice, don't say anything at all."

Family members read scriptures and the poem "Footsteps in the Sand," her favorite. We concluded with the Lord's Prayer, not "Now I Lay Me Down to Sleep." A light lunch followed at the Pickwick with more guests. Those assembled to honor Mom were slow to disperse, immersed in quiet conversations, and seemed almost hesitant to leave. Perhaps this was due to the extended periods of separation endured during the pandemic.

After lunch, the immediate family visited the Glensheen Mansion. The break on a bleak spring day was welcomed. I had not been there since our honeymoon, and our family hadn't been together since Christmas. Having three months to process Mom's death and the presence of her family and friends helped me to view the day as a celebration of her life, diminishing the sadness.

I have come to appreciate the extraordinary strength and love my mother demonstrated throughout her life, especially when I reflect on the difficulties she faced. Despite the challenges of being on the autism spectrum with neuro-atypical tendencies, at the age of twenty-one, Mom was employed and cared for three children while married to an often-unemployed alcoholic.

She became a grandmother at age thirty-two, nine months after her last child was born. Fearful of flying, she crossed the country on trains and buses to visit me. She did not express feelings like most, but I knew she loved me. Her resilience in creating stability amid these difficulties and her Catholic faith are something I more deeply appreciate now, more than I ever did as a child. Her life was a testament to her convictions in the face of personal hardships, more than mere stubbornness.

Her decision not to place me for adoption revealed quiet heroism. In her unique way, she taught me about strength, courage, and the boundless capacity of a mother's love. Her legacy continues to inspire me, and I am profoundly grateful for the life lessons she demonstrated that I have been slow to embrace, namely, patience and steadfastness. Thank you, Momma, you have had the patience of a saint, and I am so sorry for any angst I caused you and for judging you unfairly. You were right, you were not like me, and you did not think like me. I wish I had understood our differences years ago. I would have been nicer to you. But more importantly, a greater understanding would have nourished our relationship and minimized the tension. Mom, thank you for never holding our differences against me and for always accepting and forgiving me. I was too arrogant to recognize your gifts.

Replacing a fabricated story with the truth of my life in an orphanage and foster care filled the gaps of uncertainty about my mom with newfound trust. Learning how she kept me in a safe place affirmed her intentions and love for me. Unconditional love for Mom and gratitude for all who helped on her difficult journey to keep us together filled the hole in my heart that misunderstanding and mistrust had eroded.

REDUCTIONS AND REVISIONS

My fifty-one-year-old brother Vincent was struggling to stay alive on the one-year anniversary of Mom's death. Having ballooned up to 650 pounds, his heart was working overtime in the final stages of congestive heart failure and grief. He died the next day. The sorrow I experienced was the same sorrow I felt when my sister died too young; a sadness for the loss of what could have been. According to Mom, he didn't want anyone to know about his heart problems, not even me. I couldn't let on that I knew; it would have destroyed his trust with Mom.

I became the executor of his estate and enlisted the services of the agent who had helped sell Mom's house. Within a week, I accepted an offer and set in motion a cascade of events to close the escrow and his estate a year later.

I emptied Vincent's home of thirty years in five days. The overwhelming burden was lifted a bit by his ex-wife, who removed trash and emptied the refrigerator, cupboards, and cabinets. As I entered his bedroom, I recalled our last phone conversations.

"Vince, I don't know how to make your life better, but I do know when I've felt like I was drowning in sadness and out of control, it was my faith that brought me back to the surface so I could breathe again," I had told him. "I am going to send you a book that helped me, *Jesus Calling.*[25]"

That book was on his nightstand the day he died.

My son, Michael, traveled from California, and Uncle Ed drove from Saint Paul to help me with the heavy lifting, both physically and emotionally. I disposed of Vincent's belongings in the same fashion as Mom's, using online markets to sell and donating heavy stuff to folks happy to haul it away. The same friends who helped when Mom died made a repeat appearance. Their presence alleviated my sadness and helped me stay focused.

An unexpected discovery while emptying Vincent's house was discovering my stepfather Don's Army records from his time on active duty during the Korean Conflict. Typed on near-transparent onion skin paper was a report from the base psychiatrist outlining Dad's traumatic childhood as the probable contributor to his mistrust of authority and his mental health challenges. By age seventeen, Don had lived in a multitude of foster homes. He and his siblings were placed in them following the death of his father and the onset of his mother's alcoholism. As a child, I knew something was not right with Don, and eventually I distanced myself from him by moving away. Vincent had not escaped the challenges as I had.

Vince and I had a small window of opportunity to connect as siblings in a loving way following my call to wish him a happy thirty-ninth birthday. He ended the call with the following comment: "Deb, now that I can fit on a plane, I'm coming to visit you."

He had lost 200 pounds. During our visit, we got reacquainted. Sadly, we were like strangers. I had left home when he was four months old, and he had not visited me in over twenty years and was seldom around when I visited Mom. I enjoyed seeing my handsome and funny younger brother. His massive weight loss revealed the self-confidence that had been hiding under his shame. One of the more profound things he told me was, "You have no idea how much nicer people are to me since I have lost weight. Especially the people I've known for years who no longer recognize me."

Vincent sent me a thank-you gift after our visit, a hoodie with an emblem from the college I had attended. Enclosed was a thank-you note with an explanation.

"Debbie, I think your success in life happened because you got educated. I checked out the school you went to and bought the hoodie in their gift shop. I've decided I want to get an education now that I can fit in a desk and chair at school. Thank you for the nice time. Vincent."

Vince graduated from community college while working full-time night shifts, trying to make a better life for his new wife and young son. However, he did not escape the long-term effects of childhood adversities.

May 20, 2022

The light at the end of that dreary week appeared when I visited Vincent's son, Grant. After finalizing the sale of the house, I met Grant, with his mom, my ex-sister-in-law, at a restaurant near the realtor's office. I had a surprise for him: notes from his father, discovered behind school pictures proudly displayed on the living room wall. Grant had experienced tremendous loss in less than two years: his parents' divorce, moving to a new home and school, and the death of his grandma and father. My heart ached for him as I sat across from him, peering over the notes in the photo album. In that moment, I said, "Grant, do you know what day it is today?"

It had been exactly one year since I had buried Mom's ashes. I paused for a moment, waiting for eye contact, and said, "Today is Grandma's birthday. I miss her a lot, and I know you do too. Sometimes I feel incredibly sad, but not every day. I try to remember the things that make me smile when I think of her. I know it's not easy losing a parent. You will have sad days too, Grant, but as time passes, you will have fewer sad days." I looked across the booth at his mom, who had a tear in her eye, and I said, "Your mom will help you on the sad days."

Stage Four Reflections: Acceptance

The final stage of wound healing and our last quarter of life requires a response to loss. The body repairs and replaces lost tissue in the wound with less flexible scar tissue, rendering it weaker than the original tissue. Similarly, the loss of loved ones, relationships, and what and who we once were often diminishes our strength and ability to overcome overcome loss, creating a need to embrace new purposes, accept our imperfections, and adjust our expectations of ourselves and others. The pain and grief in losing my mother, siblings, and friendships over time has awakened in me greater appreciation, love, and gratitude for them.

Just as readjusting collagen fibers enhances flexibility and strengthens tissue, readjusting my attitude and expectations of myself and others to be more **accepting** and forgiving has strengthened my self-worth and personal relationships. Learning about Mom's neurodiversity increased my capacity to understand and accept the perspectives of others without judgment. The final stage of our emotional and spiritual healing requires acceptance of what we have no control over. Unlike physical healing, emotional and spiritual healing continue throughout our lives. There is always hope and possibility for more healing.

CHAPTER FIFTEEN

FINAL REFLECTIONS

JANUARY 2023

When I paused my nursing career, daily reflections on "The Lord's Prayer" guided me through a transformation—much like a butterfly emerging from its cocoon. I struggled and persevered, breaking away from the past to rediscover joy and a renewed sense of purpose. This healing experience began with a personal sense of awareness about myself, the world, others, and my creator. Since the death of my mother and brother, becoming an empty nester when Garret moved out of state, and with my last move to Sonoma County, I've experienced additional healing cycles. I've embraced a new community where I am discovering new ways to share and receive gifts of healing energy.

As this memoir ends, I realize a healing energy has guided and motivated me to release burdens and embrace gifts that shaped and enhanced my purpose and healing. I believe this energy is love, a Divine gift that inspires us to be in reciprocal relationships with each other and The Creator motivating us to offer and accept healing gifts with compassion, forgiveness, and gratitude. To participate in this exchange is to participate in nature's cycle of natural healing and to reap the benefit of recurring resilience, which empowers us for the next healing cycle.

Each healing cycle connects our body, mind, and spirit with the intention of continuing, providing a reason or purpose to face another day. With each cycle, strength is attained to meet our next challenge, reinforcing our identity as survivors with purpose, rather than as victims. Awareness of and participation in this process gradually builds resilience with each wave of woundedness. There is no fixed point in healing; it is experienced daily in recurring relationships with one another and the Divine Creator, unfolding in stages guided by our thoughts and actions.

My healing has never happened in isolation; it has always been experienced through nonjudgmental relationships, shared compassion, and the belief that we are all worthy of the gift of healing. For you, the reader, be curious, ask yourself, *what time and season am I in?* Is it a season for letting go of burdens that hinder your well-being? Or perhaps you are in a season of searching for or accepting healing gifts? Maybe you are contemplating a season of sharing your gifts, talents, and skills with others to contribute to the ongoing exchange of healing energy. Seasons come and go like cycles of woundedness and healing. May your next season include reciprocal healing, where suffering can be the catalyst for healing, enhanced resilience, and a source for contributions that spread the healing energy of love from the Divine Creator.

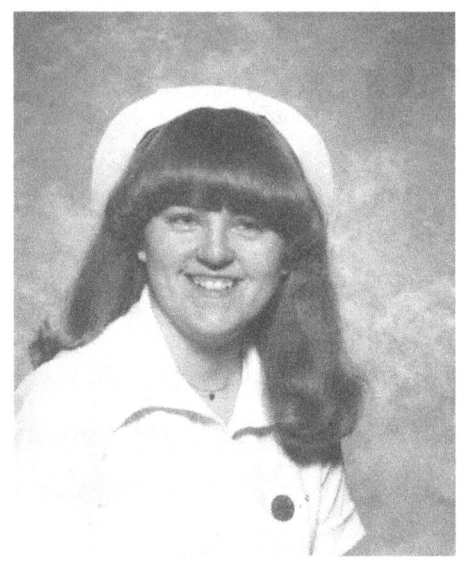

1980 College Nursing Graduation

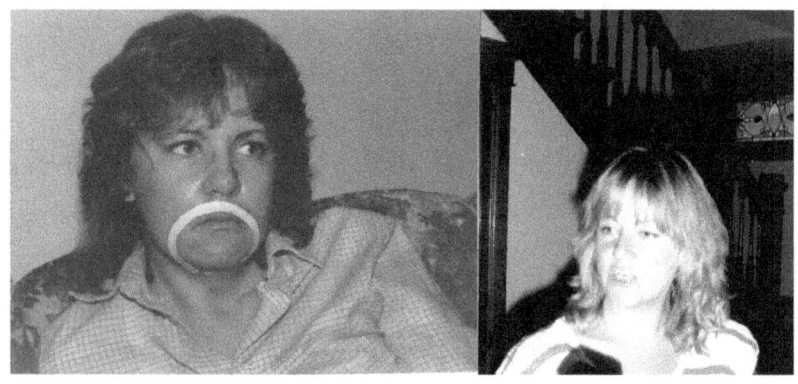

1986 after face surgery

1990s work ID

2018 PhD Graduation

Dr. Felittie and me 2025

BIBLIOGRAPHY

1. Ruffin, T. Rice, ME, Wilso, DR *Top Post Pandemic Global Health Concerns* , American Nurse vo.20 (2) Feb 2025 p. 22

2. Wallace HA, Basehore BM, Zito PM. Wound Healing Phases. [Updated 2023 Jun 12]. In: StatPearls [Internet]. Treasure Island (FL): StatPearls Publishing; 2025 Jan-. Available from: https://www.ncbi.nlm.nih.gov/books/NBK470443/

3. Shem, Samuel *House of God*, Richard Marek Publishing: New York 1978

4. Harris, TH, *I'm Okay You're Okay*, Harper and Row 1969

5. Dyer, WW, *Your Erroneous Zones*, Funk and Wagnalls, New York 1976

6. Peal, NV, *The Power of Positive Thinking*, Prentice Hall: New Jersey 1952

7. Felitti, VJ, et al., *Relationship of Childhood Abuse and Household Dysfunction to Many Leading Causes of Death in Adults: The Adverse Childhood Experience (ACE) Study* American Journal of Preventative Medicine vol. 14 (4) 1998

8. Harris, NB, *How Childhood Trauma Affects Health Across a Lifetime* TED Talk https://www.youtube.com/watch?v=95ovIJ3dsNk

9. Covey, SR. *7 Habits of Highly Effective Families* Western Publishing & Franklin Covey Racine, WI. (1997)

10. Covey, SR *7 Habits of Highly effective People* Simon and Schuster New York, NY.(1997)

11. Szyf, M., Mc Gowen, P. Meaney, M. *The Social Environment and the Epigenome* Environment and Molecular Mutagenesis 49, no1 (2008): 46-60

12. Van Der Kolk, B. *The Body Keeps the Score: Brain, Mind and Body in the Healing of Trauma* Penguin Random House: New York NY (2014)

13. Poletti, S. *From the Cradle to the Grave* Brain Medicine 2025

https://genomicpress.kglmeridian.com/view/journals/brainmed/aop/article-10.61373-bm025k.0071/article-10.61373-bm025k.0071.xml

https://scienmag.com/italian-neuroscientist-uncovers-lasting-brain-impact-of-childhood-trauma/?utm_source=bluesky-&utm_medium=jetpack_socia

14. Gwinn,C. *Cheering for the Children: Creating Pathways to Hope for Children Exposed to Trauma* Wheatmark,Inc. (2015)

15. Anandarajah, G., et al. *Spirituality and Medical Practice: Using the HOPE Questions as a Practical Tool for Spiritual Assessment.* American Family Physician, 63(1), (2001) p 81–89.

16. Puchalski, C. M.,Romer, A. L. *Taking a Spiritual History Allows Clinicians to Understand Patients More Fully.* Journal of Palliative Medicine, 3(1) (2000) p129–137. https://gwish.smhs.gwu.edu/programs/transforming-practice-health-settings/clinical-fica-tool

17. Maugans, T. A. *The SPIRITual History* Family Medicine, 5(1), (1996) p11–16.

18. Rath, Tom. *Strength Finder 2.0* Gallp Press : New York (2007)

19. Palmer, DM, *Orthopedic Nurse Practitioner as a Subspecialty: A Case Study Jan 31,2018 .https://digital.sandiego.edu/dissertations*

20. Mathew chapter nine verses 9-13 (Bible NRSV) 1989

21. www.resilientyolo.org

22. Bunnell, DL *History of Wabasha County* HH Hill & Co: Chicago

23. Dalai Lama, Tutu, D *The Book of Joy: Lasting Happiness in a Changing World.* New York: Avery (2016)

24. Gawande, A. *Being Mortal: Medicine and What Matters in the End.* New York: Metropolitan Books, 2014

25. Young, S. *Jesus Calling: Exploring Peace in His Presence* Thomas Nelson 2004

ACKNOWLEDGMENTS

A heartfelt thank you to all who encouraged me to share my story, especially Jane who is no longer with us. For those who were able to complete the first draft as reviewers, thank you for gifting me with your time, wisdom, and insight in the final phase of completing the manuscript, especially Jan Berguson, Rosemary Goodyear, Maryos Kuiper, Louis Schuster, Vincent Felitti, Rhoberta Haley, and Laurie Bayen. Tom, thank you for years of support, encouragement, guidance and advice in the first round of edits. To my dependable and loving daughter, thank you for sharing your photography and design talents. And to Jeremy, thank you for your patience through the years as we discussed the book and for your final suggestions. And lastly, the continuous source of healing energy and inspiration from my friends, family, faith community and the Devine Creator are the reasons I've been able to share a piece of my heart with my readers. Thank you

ABOUT THE AUTHOR

DR. DEBRA PALMER is the debut author of *Between Wounded and Well: Lessons in Healing,* a powerful memoir about a resilient wounded healer whose journey began as a fourteen-year-old mother. With four decades of distinguished experience as a nurse practitioner and nursing professor, Dr. Palmer has dedicated her career to advancing healthcare practices and improving patient outcomes.

Her groundbreaking collaboration with the medical community significantly contributed to pioneering the role of orthopedic nurse practitioners, helping to establish new standards of orthopedic care that continue to benefit patients today. This exceptional work earned her recognition from her peers through the California Association for Nurse Practitioners' prestigious Bridging Healthcare Needs Award. Her employer further honored her contributions with both The Everyday Hero Award and a Community Service Award, testament to her unwavering commitment to healing others.

Dr. Palmer's academic achievements reflect her dedication to excellence in nursing education and practice. She earned her Bachelor of Science in Nursing from the College of St. Scholastica and completed both her master's degree and dual doctorate degrees, a DNP and PhD in Nursing, from the University of San Diego. This extensive educational foundation has enabled her to bridge the gap between clinical practice, research, and education throughout her distinguished career.

A transplant from the Midwest, Dr. Palmer now resides in Northern California with her husband, near their adult children and grandchildren. When she's not working in her new Wellness business or writing, she finds restoration through hiking in nature and tending her garden. *Between Wounded and Well* represents her first foray into memoir writing, offering readers intimate insights into the healing journey from both deeply personal and professional perspectives.

Exclusive Free Offer for Readers of
Between Wounded and Well: Lessons in Healing

SEVEN RECURRING RESILIENCE PRACTICES TO PROMOTE POSITIVE WELL-BEING

To all readers of Between Wounded and Well: Lessons in Healing, as a heartfelt thank you for your engagement with my book and your commitment to your own healing journey, I am delighted to extend a special gift exclusively for you.

I have created a tip sheet featuring 7 essential practices for promoting positive well-being, each one thoughtfully discussed within the pages of Between Wounded and Well. These practices are drawn directly from my life experiences described in the book and are crafted to help you nurture your sense of wholeness, resilience, and vitality every day.

- Simple, actionable steps to integrate healing practices into your daily life
- Reminders from the book to inspire ongoing growth and self-care
- Accessible guidance you can revisit as often as you wish
- How to Access Your Free Tip Sheet:
- Visit my website: www.debrapalmer.com
- Look for the exclusive offer for readers of Between Wounded and Well
- Download the tip sheet and begin integrating these practices right away

Whether you are just beginning your healing journey or seeking new ways to deepen your experience, these seven resilience building practices offer practical support and encouragement. I hope this resource will bring even more value to your reading and inspire positive changes in your life.

With gratitude and encouragement,

Debra Palmer

www.ingramcontent.com/pod-product-compliance
Lightning Source LLC
Chambersburg PA
CBHW060142130626
46556CB00006B/2457